PRAISE FOR *A SYMPHONY OF CHOICES*

"*A Symphony of Choices* is a timely resource full of practical tools and real examples that will help you build the knowledge and skills to thrive in a project-driven world.

Antonio Nieto-Rodriguez, World Champion in Project Management, Thinkers50, Director PMO, PMI Fellow and Past Chair; professor, author, executive coach

"We live today in a hyperconnected world that reflects the old expression that, when a butterfly flaps its wings in the East, it causes chaos in the West, and vice versa! Gerald has written the business parable that beautifully guides you through the challenges of successfully implementing projects and initiatives. More importantly, it provides you with the tools and tips to succeed. A must-read."

Robin Speculand, Specialist in Strategy and Digital Implementation; co-author of the *Strategy Implementation Playbook* and author of the *World's Best Bank*

"If you had to choose one book on managing projects and portfolios in the new digital world, *A Symphony of Choices* by Gerald Leonard is it. Gerald provides lessons learned from the pandemic. He is real, and he knows that our personal and work buckets often combine, and he provides many tips on how to prioritize and execute your plans effectively. You will learn how to be more proactive and less reactive. Gerald will coach you on how to start using the windshield more to focus forward and anticipate what is coming around the bend. For a project management book, it is a real page-turner."

Joe Rose, Chairman, Turnberry Solutions

"Gerald's *A Symphony of Choices* definitely strikes a chord for those of us struggling to manage our customers, our bosses, our teams, and the omnipresent 'unknowns.' He takes a realistic perspective on coping with the real-world challenges that make up the juggling of expectations, time, money, and personalities. The orchestral analogy provides a simple common context that affords even the novice an opportunity to see how portfolio management can be done while at the same time providing insight for the veteran practitioner."

Carl Pritchard, 2019 PMI Global Eric Jennet
"Best of the Best" award winner

"Gerald's passion for music and expertise in project management shines in his latest book, *A Symphony of Choices*. This engaging story follows the relatable journey of one who feels overwhelmed, faces challenges, struggles with urgencies, navigates uncertainties, formulates strategies, and ultimately implements successful initiatives that help transform the organization and deliver meaningful results. The timely lessons delightfully conveyed in this approachable business parable are applicable and transferable to most any industry."

Rob Tieman, PE, PMP, Director of VDOT Project
Management; Office/Chair of AASHTO Technical
Committee on Project Management

"I highly recommend *A Symphony of Choices*. It is by far the best business book I have ever read. Gerald Leonard has given us a complete course in business management that can be adapted to any business in a most compelling story. Brilliant!"

Bobbie Stevens, PhD, Founder and CEO,
Unlimited Futures, LLC

"Executing on strategy requires effective decision-making around essential priorities and important deadlines. But management of the big picture must be in everyone's awareness, not just a task that gets handed off to a project manager. Gerald Leonard brings a fresh approach to demystifying the critical skills of project management and problem-solving for anyone in business. Mr. Leonard's gift for crafting an entertaining narrative combines with his years of expertise in corporate leadership in his insightful new book."

Paul R. Scheele, PhD, CEO of Scheele Learning Systems;
author of *Natural Brilliance* and *Drop Into Genius*

"*A Symphony of Choices* is an intersection of music meets project, program, and portfolio management. A practical read with useful tips and helpful stories to give the project professional a great resource to have on their shelf."

Dr. Michael O'Connor, 2021 PMOGA PMO Leader of the Year for the Americas and World Award Winner, 2021 PMI Eric Jenett "Best of the Best" Award Winner; Senior Research Program Director, Program Management, Medtronic

"Gerald Leonard's brilliance is that rare combination of hypercreativity, shown in both his writing and virtuoso musicianship, and high organizational, business, process, and project management skills. This book is a beautiful parable containing insights, strategies, and processes for project management directed at the achievement of big goals! I highly recommend *A Symphony of Choices*!"

Mike Rayburn, CSP, CPAE, Speaker Hall of Fame,
TED Talks; multi-award-winning artist

"*A Symphony of Choices* is an insightful, engaging, yet practical approach to executing effective decision-making around demanding priorities and essential deadlines. Gerald Leonard has done it again. He has captured an engaging story wrapped in his years of experience as a professional musician, providing wisdom that any business leader can understand and use immediately."

Bill Cates, CSP, CPAE, author of *Radical Relevance* and *Beyond Referrals*

A
SYMPHONY
OF
CHOICES

A

SYMPHONY

OF

CHOICES

How Mentorship
Taught a Manager
Decision-Making,
Project Management and
Workplace Engagement—
and Saved a Concert Season

GERALD J. LEONARD

WILEY

Published by John Wiley & Sons, Inc., Hoboken, New Jersey.
Published simultaneously in Canada.

For general information on our other products and services or for technical support, please contact our Customer Care Department within the United States at (800) 762-2974, outside the United States at (317) 572-3993 or fax (317) 572-4002.

Wiley also publishes its books in a variety of electronic formats. Some content that appears in print may not be available in electronic formats. For more information about Wiley products, visit our web site at www.wiley.com.

Library of Congress Cataloging-in-Publication Data:

Names: Leonard, Gerald J., author.
Title: A symphony of choices : how mentorship taught a manager
    decision-making, project management and workplace engagement -- and
    saved a concert season / by Gerald J. Leonard.
Description: Hoboken, New Jersey : Wiley, [2023] | Includes bibliographical
    references and index.
Identifiers: LCCN 2023008418 (print) | LCCN 2023008419 (ebook) | ISBN
    9781394197538 (hardback) | ISBN 9781394197583 (adobe pdf) | ISBN
    9781394197569 (epub)
Subjects: LCSH: Management. | Decision making. | Project management. |
    Mentoring.
Classification: LCC HD31.2 .L466 2023 (print) | LCC HD31.2 (ebook) | DDC
    658--dc23/eng/20230515
LC record available at https://lccn.loc.gov/2023008418
LC ebook record available at https://lccn.loc.gov/2023008419

Cover Design: Paul McCarthy
Cover Image: © Adobe Stock | Andrey Popov
SKY10048970_060923

CONTENTS

FOREWORD

by Antonio Nieto-Rodriguez

Projects change the world. Projects make impossible dreams possible.

The behavioral and social sciences endorse the idea that there are a few ways of working and collaborating that are particularly motivating and inspiring for people working on a project. These are that a project should have ambitious goals, a higher purpose, and a clear deadline. You have probably noticed that what people tend to remember most clearly from their entire careers are the projects they work on – often the successful ones, but also the failed ones.

According to recent research, the number of individuals working in project-based roles will increase from 66 million (in 2017) to 88 million (forecast 2027). And the value of economic activity worldwide that is project-oriented will grow from $12 trillion (in 2013) to $20 trillion (forecast 2027).[1] Those are millions of projects requiring millions of project managers per year.

This is what I describe as the Project Economy, a term I conceived in 2018 when working on my earlier book *The Project Revolution: How to Succeed in a Project-Driven World*.

This silent disruption is impacting not only organizations but also the very nature of work and our entire professional lives. The traditional one-company career path of previous generations is now a distant memory. Today, people happily and fruitfully change jobs and employers a number of times during their careers. I believe that this trend will accelerate and that professional careers will become a sequence of projects. Another notable trend related to this is the growth in self-employment. They will be effective in managing a port-folio of projects.

A GLOBAL REVOLUTION

The more you look, the more projects you will see. On my desk, I have a bushel of examples.

For example, in December 2016, the US Senate unanimously approved the Program Management Improvement and Accountability Act (PMIAA),[2] which will enhance accountability and best prac-tices in project and program management throughout the US federal government. The PMIAA will reform federal program management policy in three important ways: creating a formal job series and career path for program and project managers in the federal government, developing a standards-based program and project management policy across the federal government that recognizes the essential role of executive sponsorship and engagement by designating a senior exec-utive in federal agencies to be responsible for program and project management policy and strategy, sharing knowledge of successful approaches to program and project management through an inter-agency council on program and project management.

In the UK, on January 6, 2017, the Association for Project Management was awarded a Royal Charter.[3] The receipt of a Royal Charter marks a significant achievement in the evolution of project management and will have positive implications for those who make, and seek to make, a career in this field. The charter recognizes the project management profession, rewards the association that cham-pions its cause, and provides opportunities for those who practice its disciplines.

The Richards Group is the largest independently owned ad agency in the United States, with billings of $1.28 billion, revenue of

$170 million, and more than 650 employees. Stan Richards, its founder, and CEO, removed almost all of its management layers and job titles, leaving only that of project manager.[4]

In another example, in 2016 Nike was looking to fill a vacancy at its European headquarters. The job description was "Corporate Strategy & Development Manager for the European, Middle East & Africa (EMEA) Region." Such a job would traditionally entail strategic planning, market analysis, and competitive intelligence competencies. To my surprise, instead the job was described as "project management." This meant that Nike was looking for someone who could implement transversal and strategic projects for its strategy function. This was a clear shift of focus and culture: from planning and day-to-day activities to implementation and projects. And Nike is not alone – I have seen similar job descriptions for strategy functions at UPS, Amazon, and others.

IN THE PROJECT ECONOMY, WE ARE ALL PROJECT MANAGERS

For centuries, learning was achieved by memorizing hefty books and mountains of written material. Today, the leading educational systems, starting from an early age, apply the concept of teaching projects. Applying theories and experimenting through projects has proven to be a much better learning method, and soon it will become the norm.

Not so long ago, professional careers were made in only one organization. Throughout the 20th century, most people worked for a single company. Today we are likely to work for several companies, and at some point we will most probably become self-employed, working primarily on projects. This sort of career is best approached as a set of projects in which we apply the lessons we have learned from previous jobs, companies, and industries while developing ourselves for our next career move, often not known in advance.

The emergence of projects as the economic engine of our times is silent but incredibly disruptive and powerful. And this massive

disruption is impacting not only the way organizations are managed –
every aspect of our lives is becoming a set of projects.

A SYMPHONY OF CHOICES

Juggling multiple projects has become one of our major challenges,
both as individuals as well as organizations, in our private and in our
professional lives. Gerald Leonard's book *A Symphony of Choices* is a
timely resource full of practical tools and real examples that will help
you build the knowledge and skills to thrive in a project-driven world.

Following the inspiration from the bestselling book *The Goal* by
Eliyahu M. Goldratt, Gerald tells us a business fable of a musician
who is given the opportunity to become the personnel manager for
the symphony he is playing with. From the first page of the book, the
story manages to be both engaging and enlightening as it teaches us
the principles of project portfolio management.

> *"There are fewer 'low-cost' ways of working more inclusive, impactful, motivat-*
> *ing and inspiring than being part of a project with an ambitious goal, a higher*
> *purpose, and a clear fixed deadline."*
>
> – Antonio Nieto-Rodriguez

PREFACE

After writing my first two books, *Culture Is the Bass* and *Workplace Jazz,* I realized there was something missing. I provided guidelines for company cultures and high-performing agile teams, but I had not discussed how to manage projects and portfolios. I had created books around the people, and now I needed to consider the processes of effective decision-making and project portfolio management (PPM).

I began to dive into other books on the subject. While they had a lot of great information, charts, and technical information, they were essentially . . . boring. They provided tools but in a very stiff and institutional manner. I didn't want to do that. The world didn't need another tome that people wouldn't read and only stuck on their shelves to be seen by others on a Zoom call.

This had to be different. Something that captured the reader and brought them through the processes of effective decision-making and PPM without putting them to sleep. This book needed to create a story from which the reader could follow and learn.

Then the pandemic hit, which meant I had more time to reflect on this issue, as people's normal everyday way of doing things was severely disrupted. People began working at home, and team meetings became virtual. People were forced to shift what they were doing, but they found themselves in difficult spots because they didn't have a plan. Projects went off the rails or were canceled because there was no mechanism for making the shift. It became overwhelming.

In addition, new challenges and projects arose. Again, team leaders had to adapt to changing landscapes and find ways to get their teams to perform. New goals were established, but the process of achieving those goals became a hindrance.

If you were used to having a morning meeting and then walking over to your teammate in the next office to ask a question, and all of that was taken away, how can you adapt? In addition, the way in which projects were handled changed. The analog way of things now was shifting to digital. As a consultant, even I had to adjust and meet these new challenges. The difference I observed between the companies that survived and those that didn't was how they handled making effective decisions and if they had PPM processes that were easy to follow. With a strong understanding and process in place, they could handle whatever challenges they encountered. They could easily pivot when it was called for and create new projects with confidence and ease.

I had created an online program to teach PPM, which has been very successful, but how could I convert that knowledge into a book people would want to read? I fell back on the adage that authors know all too well. Write what you know.

I know PPM not only from a consulting position but from a practical one. I worked with a law firm and other large companies to create a PPM system that worked. I had those stories I could share.

The second piece is my musical background. It is the story of my soul, and I have used it in my first two books to illustrate culture and agile project management in a successful manner.

I still struggled with the last piece of the puzzle – the structure. How could I bring my life as a PPM expert and my life as a musician together into one cohesive story?

I reread the book *The Goal* by Eliyahu Goldratt and Jeff Cox. It is a business fable, and while it is over 20 years old, it still is engaging. Its purpose is to transform management thinking. I was on to something.

I began thinking about a business fable, a story that would be both engaging and would teach the principles of PPM. It was time for me to dig deep into my own life and find the storyline. And so Jerry, the protagonist, was born. He is a musician who is given the opportunity to become the personnel manager for the symphony he is playing with. He becomes quickly overwhelmed and must figure out how to meet all the expectations of his job. In the background are serious marital problems as well as an injury. He finds he is juggling multiple balls, and he is about to drop all of them.

He looks up his professor from college who taught business management. Dr. Carl Richardson agrees to help Jerry for the price of a cup of coffee. We follow Jerry's progress, and we learn directly from Dr. Richardson the steps of PPM. The lessons he teaches Jerry are drawn directly from my online course. I draw upon actual experiences in both my business life and my personal one.

At the end of the book, I consolidate all the lessons Dr. Richardson teaches for easy reference and practical application. My goal is to show how these principles are applied even when there are challenges, such as a pandemic. Jerry's confidence builds, and eventually he is juggling only one or two balls (projects) at a time, and he has developed a system of prioritization and execution. This isn't easy or perfect, and he has to adjust his strategies when they aren't working.

I include parts of his personal life because this is the way in which we exist. We don't shut out our personal lives when we are engaged in business. He learns to use the lessons acquired from Dr. Richardson and begins applying them to his whole life. In the end, he is happier and more goal-oriented. He isn't merely reacting to emergencies; he is predicting where they can occur and mitigating them. This lowers his stress, boosts his confidence, and improves his newly minted career and his family life.

I hope you enjoy reading this as much as I enjoyed writing it. I would love to receive your feedback and hear your stories about your journey.

CHAPTER 1

THE RIGHT PEOPLE AND THE RIGHT TIME

The orchestra was warming up and preparing for the season's last concert. I always liked the chaos of sound as people warmed up their instruments and practiced those passages and runs one last time before the performance. Mixed into the cacophony of musical instruments were the conversations of the audience. People caught up with old friends, talking about their lives and children. Some discussed their jobs or where they planned to go after the concert. Others sat silently, reading the conductor's notes about the evening's performance, including the history of the pieces and the composers who wrote them.

It was a time of building anticipation until the moment the concertmaster rose from their seat, and the orchestra and audience become silent, waiting for the first oboist to play their perfect tone for the rest of the orchestra to match. The lights dimmed, and the conductor waited a couple of moments before stepping out into the stage lights. He took a couple of deep breaths and wiped the sweat from his brow as he listened for his heartbeat. This beat would be his guide for crossing the stage to his podium. It was his baseline for the downbeat and every subsequent beat that came after.

All of this was happening as I flipped through my music, making sure it was in order. I rosined my bow and checked that the peg was secure on the floor at my feet. The point had found its groove so that my instrument didn't slide from my hands during the performance.

My mind should have been focused on the music and only the music, but I was distracted. I had just been notified at the afternoon's dress rehearsal that I had been selected as the new orchestra manager. Up to the moment I heard, I didn't really feel I had a chance. I had been in the symphony for 20 years, and so I had the experience as a musician, and I had been on the orchestra committee, a group that spoke for the needs and wants of the symphony members. However, I wasn't sure that qualified me to be the orchestra manager. It was a paid position with specific responsibilities, and this coming year, of all years, was going to be challenging.

I thought of a number of other symphony members who would have been qualified, or they could have been hired outside the symphony. The hiring committee decided that I was their first choice, not only because of my experience as a musician but because I had a few ideas of changes I wanted to implement in the coming year.

"We're so excited you are the new orchestra manager, Jerry," said Cindy Wittaker, the first bassoonist. "We loved your ideas about direct deposit for the musicians and upgrading our music distribution."

"Thanks," I replied. I had a heavy feeling in my stomach. "I'm really shocked you chose me, but I hope to do my best."

"We know you'll do great," replied Cindy.

I thought about all I needed to do before the next season. The next season was the 100th anniversary of the symphony. No pressure at all. I had not seen the program layout for the season yet, but knowing our maestro, it was going to be over the top, not only musically but logistically. The maestro loved large pieces with many musicians, and the symphony often had to rent instruments and hire extra musicians. I was sure this coming season would be no exception.

Unfortunately, there wasn't any list of musicians to be passed on to me from the previous manager. I needed to create a database from scratch and add musicians as substitutes for concerts throughout the year. In addition, I needed to set up auditions for vacant contracted musicians for the following year as well. The summer was going to be a busy time, and I only hoped I had the skills needed to put it all together.

One of the difficult parts of hiring musicians as substitutes is that I would hire them sight unseen or, in this case, sound unheard. I would have to get recommendations from other musicians for people to call. In some cases, I would call people the day before the first rehearsal if someone called in sick. How would I determine that they had the chops to play and that they were reliable enough to show up on time and be prepared? If the musician didn't show up or wasn't symphony caliber, I would be the one to answer for it, so I needed to figure it out – and fast.

The maestro stepped onto the stage, and there was thunderous applause. The maestro held a hand to us to acknowledge us, and we stood. Well, at least those seated stood. The bass section was already standing.

I mentally pushed all the distractions from my mind. It was time to be focused on the music and worry about managing later. The maestro raised his baton, and I prepared my bow for the first downbeat of Beethoven's Fifth Symphony. The baton lowered, and we were off to another magical live music experience, sure to have the patrons chattering for days to come.

★ ★ ★

At intermission, my wife approached me with that look I had learned to dread.

"I just heard from Sally that you got the position as orchestra manager," Laura said. "Why didn't you tell me?"

"Well, I just found out this afternoon," I replied. "I had to grab a quick sandwich and change before the concert. I'm sorry that I didn't have time to talk to you about it."

"We talked about this, Jerry. I didn't think it was a good idea because the pay is low, and you don't have the time."

As I remembered the conversation, it was Laura who told me it was not a good idea. The symphony provided me with such a wonderful opportunity to perform and express my creative talents that when someone nominated me for the position, I was honored.

"But I do have time," I responded. "This would actually supplement my income, not take away from it."

"What experience do you have managing a symphony? You are a musician, not a business person."

She had a point there, but I had not had time to process what I needed to do to make up for my shortfall of experience.

"Can we talk about this after the concert? I need to get back on the stage."

"Can you turn down the position?" she asked. She wasn't letting it go.

"I suppose I could, but I really don't want to. I really need to get on stage," I pleaded.

Laura crossed her arms and snapped, "Fine."

The most technical part of the concert was in the second half, and now I had my wife to contend with in addition to the pressure of figuring out what I needed to do as the orchestral manager. The orchestra members returned to their seats, just as they had at the beginning of the concert; they rosined their bows, warmed their instruments, and practiced tricky passages one last time before the performance.

As the maestro took his position on the podium, a thought occurred to me. In college, I had taken some business classes, and there was a teacher, Carl Richardson, who had left an impression on me. In college, my focus had been on music performance and education, but I really got a lot out of his classes. He might be able to give me some advice on how I would manage the orchestra and all of the things I needed to accomplish this year. I made a mental note as the maestro raised his arms, ready to give the orchestra their downbeat. All eyes were locked on him, and everyone was holding their breath, including the audience.

The baton in his hand reached upwards and then down, and the orchestra began to play. It was amazing how much control the conductor had over the orchestra. He decided the tempos and the volume; he gave people cues on when to come in. All of this was accomplished with his hands, arms, facial expressions, eye contact, and even his posture. He managed the music, and I thought as the music flowed before my eyes that I needed to be a conductor in my own right as the orchestra manager.

★ ★ ★

The next day, I met with my old professor, Dr. Richardson.

"I am so glad you could squeeze a lunch in with me," I said. "I am just a little overwhelmed with this new position I have, and I remembered you taught me about managing projects. I took notes, I promise; I just never knew I would need them."

"I'm always glad to help out a former student," Dr. Richardson replied as he sipped his tea. "So you have plunged into the world of portfolio management."

"Well, I got a position as the orchestra manager, although now I'm not sure it was the smartest move."

"How so?"

"I'm overwhelmed. I have so much to do, and there are these timelines I have to do them in. The former orchestra manager quit the symphony, so I feel like I'm starting from scratch. Why did you say portfolio management?" I asked.

"Because, from what you described, that is exactly what you're doing. Think of it like your concerts. You have this program you're performing. In that program are pieces of music you're going to play. And each of the pieces requires certain musicians to play them. You following me?"

I pulled out a small notebook and began taking notes. "Yes, go on."

"Each of those are projects that you have to manage. The choice of the program. The choice of the music and then getting that music. Picking and hiring musicians. All of those are parts of portfolio management."

"Okay, I get you so far."

"Here's a diagram for you to keep that helps demonstrate the different levels of PPM," said Dr. Richardson as he passed a piece of paper to me. (See Figure 1.1.)

"As you see, there are three levels, and you will be involved in each of them.

"Let's start off at the highest level, the portfolio management circle. Here you'll be dealing with the higher parts of the organization. In your case, it would be the board of directors, the orchestra conductor, the director of the symphony, and so on. You'll discuss the season, the

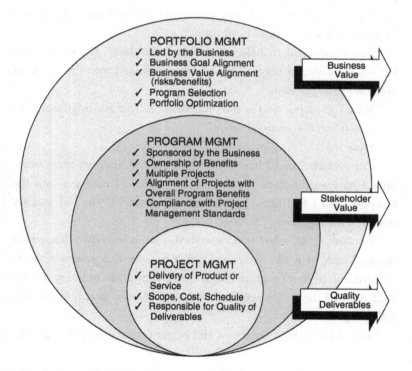

Figure 1.1 What's the difference between PPM, PgM, and PM?

programs, and any other project you'll be doing with the symphony. Do you have new things you want to implement?"

"I do want to fix the way the musicians get paid. Right now, it takes two signatures, and sometimes musicians have to wait for their checks to arrive in the mail. It's a real pain."

"So, at the portfolio management level, you might propose your changes and how you plan to roll them out."

"I want the symphony to move to direct deposit so musicians can get paid on the date of the concert."

"Great, so once you propose that project and get it approved, you would move down to the next level of program management. You would have the blessing of the director and board to implement this new program, and you would then share that with the musicians. You would explain how that process would go and what you needed from them to make it happen. You would make sure that there was a connection between the musicians and the payroll."

"Okay, I'm following you so far," I admitted. Some of the pressure was beginning to release from my shoulders.

"Then this is followed by the project management level. This is where the magic happens. You're responsible for the deliverables and making sure everything works as it's supposed to. The musicians play the concert, and they have their money by the end of the day. You'll continue at this level for each concert, making sure the process goes smoothly, and you'll have to onboard new musicians into the system as they're hired."

"That totally makes sense," I said as I fastidiously made notes.

"That's just one project. As the orchestra manager, you'll be handling multiple projects at once."

"I know; that's what's overwhelming me," I admitted.

"You need to take time and prioritize. What projects need to be done first? Once you've done that, you need to figure out at what level you'll be beginning. If it's not a new project but is one being handed to you to manage, then you may not need to begin at the portfolio level. Instead, you'd be at the program level and figure out what you need to know, have in place, and what resources you'll need. Then you can move to the project management level. Right now, it sounds like you have both new projects and ongoing projects you want to implement. My advice is to write each of them down, figure out a rough timeline for them, and begin figuring out what you'll need to begin managing them."

I sipped my coffee. Perhaps I needed a spreadsheet, or maybe I could use some software to do it.

"Is there some sort of software I can use to manage all of this?" I asked.

"Yes, there are all sorts of programs you could use," Dr. Richardson replied. "But first, I think you need to dive deeper into what are the best practices of portfolio management. This will help you tremendously moving forward."

"Are there books or articles you might recommend?" I asked.

"Sure, here are a few articles and books that a friend of mine, Gerald, who's an expert in project portfolio management, shared with me."

- What is the difference between projects, programs, and portfolios? https://www.pmworld360.com/what-is-the-difference-between-projects-programs-and-portfolios/
- 5 Secrets of strategic growth using portfolio management principles https://www.pmworld360.com/5-secrets-of-strategic-growth-using-portfolio-management-principles/
- 5 Steps for managing unrealistic expectations https://www.pmworld360.com/5-steps-for-managing-unrealistic-expectations/
- Culture Is the Bass: 7 Steps to Creating High Performing Teams https://www.amazon.com/dp/B07YMP3Q2Z
- Strategic Leadership of Portfolio and Project Management: Bridging the Gaps Between Setting and Executing Strategy https://www.businessexpertpress.com/books/strategic-leadership-portfolio-and-project-management/

"He also has an online program. You can complete it on your own time, and it can really help you. I wish I had more time to give you as you learn this process, but I'm swamped right now. You could take some classes on it, but I would assume an online program would be better for your budget and your time."

"Yes, it would," I agreed.

You can find the online program here, Ascending to the APEX of the Project Management Ladder: Demystifying Project Portfolio Management and Building a Winning Game Plan for Becoming a PPM Expert: https://geraldjleonard.teachable.com/p/the-apex-of-project-management

"I can be a resource as you have questions or need a little guidance," Dr. Richardson added.

"That would be fantastic. How about I pay you in some comp tickets for you and your wife this coming season?"

"That would be outstanding," Dr. Richardson replied.

Dr. Richardson's Tips

- Identify ideal candidates to manage the organization's project portfolio.
- Understand the difference between project, program, and portfolio management.
- Consider the value portfolio management can deliver to your organization.
- "But first, you need to dive deeper into the best practices of portfolio management. This will help you tremendously moving forward."

CHAPTER 2

CHOOSING YOUR PORTFOLIO

As I entered the symphony office, I thought about all that I had learned so far, and while I felt overwhelmed, I believed that I had a structure that I could now follow. I scheduled a meeting with the director to go over the upcoming season and see what his ideas were.

Maestro Fernando's back was to me as I knocked on his open office door. He had a set of headphones on and was conducting the music spread before him on an oversized music stand.

He must have felt my presence because he turned around and switched off the turntable.

"Hey, Jerry," said Fernando. "I'm sorry. I was going through the second movement of the *Firebird Suite*."

"Oh, I love that piece," I replied. "Are we playing it next season?"

"You didn't get a copy of next year's season? You should have said something," Fernando replied as he rifled through one of over a dozen stacks of paper. If anyone needed some portfolio management, it was Fernando. I didn't feel I was in the position to suggest it. Not because I lacked a firm grasp on the concept; it was more that Maestro Fernando was not known for graciously taking advice.

"Here," he said as he handed me a list of concerts scribbled on two sheets of notebook paper. I looked at all the pieces he wanted to add and began panicking a bit. There were a lot of big pieces that required a lot of players. There were sequences of numbers under each piece.

"What are those numbers?" I pointed to the page: Wagner, Prelude to *Die Meistersinger von Nürnberg*; Ravel, *La valse* (Commissioned Piece); Stravinsky, *The Firebird Suite* (1919 version).

2+1, 2, 2, 2, 4, 3, 3, 1

12, 12, 12, 10, 8

1 timp, 1 tri, 1 cym

Harp

"You've never seen that notation?" asked Fernando with a slightly annoyed tone. "Are you sure you're ready for this?"

Maestro Fernando wasn't on the committee to choose an orchestral manager, nor was he a decision-maker; that was left to the board. I don't believe I was his first choice. We had always been friendly to Fernando, but because I had been on the Orchestra Committee, he and I had bumped heads on a couple of items, such as breaks during rehearsal. His view had been that we needed to continue playing, and they might let the musicians out a little early if they covered all the pieces, but that rarely happened. In fact, he was renowned for going overtime, which meant time and a half for every minute we went past the designated time.

"To be honest, I'm just learning; I'd appreciate any help you can provide me," I answered.

"Well, I don't have time to teach you how to be an orchestra manager. Those numbers refer to the number of players we will need for each piece."

That would be helpful when creating a budget for the year. It would be hard to gauge what special instruments like a saxophone would cost, as they were not contracted players, but at least I could build a range into the budget that I would submit to the board of directors.

I looked over the entire season. There were six regular concerts, four chamber concerts with a new string quartet in residence, and a series of in-school concerts. This year we were going to do concerts with the local choral society. I always enjoyed these concerts; the choir was close to two hundred strong, and the concerts were the highlights of the Christmas and Easter seasons.

Two of the concerts had empty spots in their lineup. "What pieces are we playing here and here?" I asked.

"I thought Sam would have told you already," said Fernando. "We have commissioned two new pieces by Kimberly Goodwich for our Masterwork concerts. These pieces are to honor our centennial. They are not completed yet, and so they don't have titles."

Sam Colbern was the symphony director. He dealt with all the business aspects of the symphony. I had not had a chance to talk to Sam before meeting Fernando, and now I regretted that a bit. Sam was the one who had made the decision to hire me for the position.

"Do we know the instrumentation for those pieces?" I asked.

"Not yet, but I will make sure you have the numbers in plenty of time before rehearsals."

That wasn't comforting for two reasons. The first was the most immediate; I had to create a budget to submit to Sam and the board. I didn't want to pad the numbers, so I would have to ask the board to be aware that there could be a higher cost if we needed many more instruments.

The second issue was that if there were a need for a number of extra musicians, it might be difficult to find them. I was usually booked for gigs six months to a year in advance. Finding someone last minute could be difficult and expensive because I wouldn't have much negotiating room if we were desperate.

"I'm going to have to set up auditions this summer," I said. "I wanted to make a few changes."

Again, I saw a small wince on the maestro's face. "And those are?"

"Well, I want to make them blind auditions. You know, I would put up a screen, and they would be given a number. There have been complaints in the past that auditions were not fair because the committee could see the musicians."

"Who said that?" replied the maestro. "Are people saying I'm not impartial?"

I knew this was going to be a sore spot with Fernando, so I was prepared. "All of the major symphonies — New York, Chicago, Boston — have blind auditions. I just want our symphony to be up to date with the trends of bigger symphonies."

I knew this would appeal to Fernando's ego. He felt our symphony, which was a midsized orchestra, could play as well as any other major symphony. I actually applauded that sentiment because it pushed us to play better.

"Okay, but I still want to have last say on who the contract musicians are," replied Fernando. "I am the music director, and that is my job."

"Of course," I said. "I will put together a process for that as quickly as possible."

"What else do you want to change?"

"Well, I'd like us to audition for sub musicians. I also would like to be able to pay them a little more."

"I don't mind auditioning sub musicians, and maybe some of the people who don't get a contract position could be considered for a sub position. But let me be clear — I don't deal with money at all. I don't want to know about it or talk about it. That is between you and Sam to figure out."

I made a mental note not to bring it up again with Fernando, but it could tie my hands a bit. I saw a number of specialty instruments and larger ensembles on the season schedule, and they might be hard to fill if I didn't have the budget for them. It was something I would have to talk to Sam about. The maestro wouldn't care what it cost as long as a position was filled with the highest-caliber musician possible. It fell to me to figure out how that would happen.

"I hate to cut our meeting short, but I need to get to lunch with some of the donors. I don't really like these types of events, but Sam often reminds me that without donors, subscribers, and endowments, I would not have a job."

"That was pretty much it for now," I said, even though there were a few more items I had hoped to discuss. "Can we meet again soon to talk through some other items?"

"Sure, but be aware. In three weeks, after the meeting with the board, I will be gone guest conducting in the Hamptons for about five weeks. You can send me emails, I suppose. I'll be back in town about two weeks before we begin our first rehearsal. I guess you'll need to schedule those auditions in the next couple of weeks before I leave town."

I panicked; my heart beat hard and I broke out in a sweat. I had wanted to do auditions in July, but now I would have to schedule them sometime in the next couple of weeks. I needed to contact Dr. Richardson about how best to organize this audition. But first, Sam and I needed to speak.

MEETING WITH SAM

I waited at the table for Sam to arrive. I already had a cold pint of ale waiting for him. Even though it was just past noon, I knew Sam would appreciate it.

Sam McPhee had become the executive director a couple of years ago. He came from a business background of working at places like Nike and Pro-Star. His background wasn't in music, and while he seemed to have an appreciation for classical music, he didn't really understand musicians and their special temperaments.

This often put him at odds with Fernando, one arguing artistic integrity and the other dollars and cents. Sam and I hit it off at an after-concert party, sharing similar tastes in food and drink, and we both liked playing golf. He would often invite me for a round at the local country club, followed up with lunch, usually his treat. Today I was paying the bill because I needed his attention and advice.

Sam was my direct report, and so I needed to make him happy with my work if I expected to continue in my position. My wife was not happy with my choice to take the position in the first place; she felt

I was in over my head and that it was going to stress me out. She wasn't totally wrong, but I wanted to give it my best effort before throwing in the towel.

One of the things I liked about Sam was his bright smile and high-spirited nature. He loved telling jokes and was always positive about things no matter what was happening. I wished I had his eternal optimism. I hoped some of it would rub off on me today.

Sam walked in, with his bald head and his ruddy complexion. He had no hair now, but I could imagine locks of red hair in his youth. He had grown up in Scotland, and even though he had lived in the United States longer than he had in Scotland, he still had a significant accent.

He sat down in the booth and shook my hand warmly.

"Good to see you, Jerry." As he sat down, he looked at the frosting pint in front of him. "Is this for me?"

"It is!"

"You know me so well." Sam took a few sips and wiped the foam from his mustache.

The waitress came by and we gave her our order. By the time she walked away, Sam's glass was almost empty.

"Do you want another one?"

"Of course I do, but I want to be able to drive back to the office, so I need to pace myself."

We chuckled.

"How do you like your job so far?"

"Well, I'm trying to figure it all out," I admitted. "I appreciate the opportunity, and I'm trying my best to get organized. I'm unclear what you need of me and timelines and such."

"Oh, no worries," said Sam with his eternal optimism. "You'll figure it out."

"Yeah . . . I wish there was a guidebook or something," I chuckled. "My biggest challenge is the upcoming board meeting. They'll be expecting a report from me about the season's budget, and I won't have exact numbers."

"Well, how close will you be?"

"There are some pieces that haven't even been written yet, so I won't know the personnel needs of them. I don't have any budgets for the quartet in residence. Also, I don't have any budget for the in-school concerts because I don't have a list of how many there will be or what the personnel requirements will be."

"All great concerns. We can fill in the gaps with last year's budget for now. What numbers do we know?"

There was that eternal optimism. I handed him the sheet with the concerts and the personnel numbers. I was pretty sure he cursed under his breath, and his face turned a cherry color.

"This is absolutely ridiculous. He knows we were a little short on donations and ticket sales last year," said Sam in an angry tone. "If we submit these numbers, there is a good chance that the board may vote for a pay cut. Maybe I will have that second beer."

He cursed under his breath, but I couldn't quite catch the words.

"A pay cut?" I asked. "No! We are barely paid what we're worth now, and I was going to ask for a small raise for the orchestra."

"Well, then I would say we will have to figure out ways to cut our costs," Sam said. "Even if they don't feel the cut this year, next year they will if we're too far over budget."

This was becoming worse by the moment. I was glad that I had a meeting with Dr. Richardson tomorrow. I needed to get organized and get my head wrapped around program management, or I'd be sunk.

We finished our lunch, and I grabbed the ticket before he could.

"Come on, you're my employee now," said Sam.

"I know, but I need your guidance on this, so I don't mind paying."

"Don't worry, Jerry, you got this. I know better than anyone that Fernando can be difficult to deal with, especially when it comes to money, but I have your back. Make sure I have to budget in enough time, and I can fill in the gaps. You'll get the hang of this, I promise."

As I walked to my car, I hoped Sam was right. Perhaps Laura was right; maybe I did take on too much. Even though Sam seemed confident in my skills, he had not provided much about how I should prioritize my time and what projects needed to happen first.

Tomorrow was a new day, and I hoped Dr. Richardson could help me, or at least point me in the right direction.

MEETING WITH MENTOR

"Thank you so much for meeting with me, Dr. Richardson," I said. "This is all a little overwhelming."

"No worries," Richardson said. "My wife and I appreciate the tickets for next season, and I never mind someone else paying for my gourmet coffee addiction."

I told Richardson about my meetings with Sam and Fernando. He listened, nodded his head, and scribbled a couple of notes.

When I was done, he took a big sip of coffee.

"You're right; there is a lot of material to consider," said Richardson. "Just take a deep breath and relax. There are a number of things that could sidetrack you from your main goal, which sounds like the upcoming budget meeting. Do you remember when I talked about portfolios in my class?"

I grinned and shrugged. "To be honest, I never imagined I'd be in the position that I am in now. Can you give me a little refresher?"

Richardson chuckled. "No problem." He took a couple more sips of his coffee while he gathered his thoughts. He opened up a folder he had brought and handed me some papers.

"One of the key ways to organize a portfolio of projects is to organize them by what's known as a portfolio mix or categorization. This portfolio mix contains three buckets. One is transforming the business, another growing the business, and finally running the business. So think about your orchestra. You want to break the projects in the portfolio into three categories – transforming the symphony, growing the symphony, and running the symphony. You following me so far?"

"Yeah, some of it is coming back to me."

"The transforming part of the symphony project can be projects like televising the symphony orchestra on major television, or having a very famous conductor or composer write a premiere piece just for that orchestra."

"Most of the things are happening this year," I mused.

"To grow the symphony," Richardson continued, "you could find ways to cut costs by streamlining a process or reducing paperwork, making it faster for symphony musicians to get paid. You may even decide to obtain two additional endowments that will add funds to the orchestra's budget."

"I do want to make paying symphony members easier by switching us over to direct deposit."

"Finally, running the orchestra portion, you could develop projects related to keeping the symphony running smoothly by having a database of symphony musicians and alternates who can quickly be called upon."

"I want to streamline getting musicians their music sooner and prevent parts from being lost. My plan is to work with the symphony librarian, Reggie, to digitize the music. Would that fit in the running portion?"

"Yes, absolutely. You're getting it."

"But how do I prioritize these things? I mean, I could organize them, but what do I do first?"

Richardson pointed at a paper in front of me. (See Figure 2.1.)

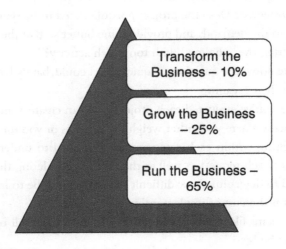

Figure 2.1   Categorizing investment types.

"Figure out what pieces need to be in place or created to execute. Once you have a list of projects that are categorized based on the transform, grow, and run categorization, you will need to determine and evaluate how you can execute those projects. First, you want to evaluate what projects are currently under way, and then you'll want to weed out any projects that are not in line with the overall strategy for the orchestra this season."

I was a bit nervous. I didn't want to take up too much of Dr. Richardson's time, but at the same time, I was feeling lost.

"I feel like I'm monopolizing your time," I said. "Do you want me to pay you anything?"

"Yes, you can buy me another cup of coffee," Richardson said. "But in the meantime, I want you to consider some questions as you begin to organize your project portfolio. One is how many projects can the symphony absorb at any given time?"

"I'm not sure," I said. "Since this is my first year doing it."

"Perhaps that's a good question for Sam then."

As Richardson talked, I scribbled down notes on a small steno notebook I had brought.

"Here are some other questions to add to that. Does the symphony have the capacity to deliver the selected portfolio of projects that are being considered? Does the project portfolio need to be synchronized to adjust to the demands and provide some buffer so that the orchestra is not getting overwhelmed with too much activity?"

I wrote down the questions as quickly as I could, barely having time to absorb their meaning.

"Once you've evaluated each project, you can create a simple valuation process where you either weigh the projects or you use a subjective weighing within each category; we also need to understand the urgency of each request as well as the risk of completing the project. You need to determine how difficult the project will be to implement and what is the cost of implementing the project."

"This seems like a lot," I said. "Will I have to figure all of this out before the budget?"

"Much of it, yes, but there are tools that can be used to help stream-line this process. To begin with, you are creating your portfolio for your own use. So you can keep it simple and use a spreadsheet. I also have a friend London who has a tool called Transparent Choice. It's a very easy tool to use for managing a portfolio of projects and helps you make decisions about which ones to execute first. You can have other members of the orchestra committee weigh in on which proj-ects they think should happen first. This helps with buy-in and execu-tion because you are establishing a team and not taking all the tasks on for yourself."

"That would be terrific. What was the name of that again?" I asked.

"Don't worry; I can provide you a link, and we can discuss that next time when you have a look at it."

"I'll go grab you that coffee," I said. While the barista steamed the milk and poured the espresso into the cup, I received a text from Dr. Richardson.

I sat down with our fresh lattes, and Dr. Richardson had another little stack of papers in front of him.

"I know you're really nervous about submitting your budget request to the board. There are a couple of tools you can use that we talked about in class that you probably don't remember."

My cheeks burned a little, and I tried not to make eye contact. He pushed the papers over to me.

"One of the tools is the portfolio roadmap, and the other one is a cost-benefit analysis." (See Figures 2.2 and 2.3.)

I looked at the large chart on the first page.

"For the portfolio, the roadmap is really an investment roadmap that provides short-, medium-, and long-term views of how the projects will be laid out and which projects will get done first. The roadmap facilitates dialogue and helps build agreement with an organization regarding the funding required for the projects to be completed and the resources required or resource allocation plan as it aligns with the overall goals and objective for the symphony."

I looked over the map of objectives and initiatives.

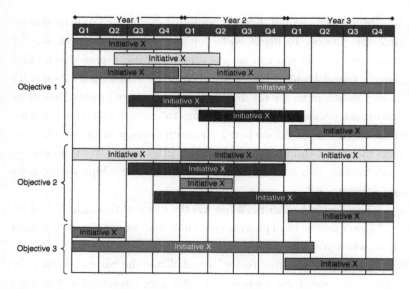

Figure 2.2   Portfolio roadmap.

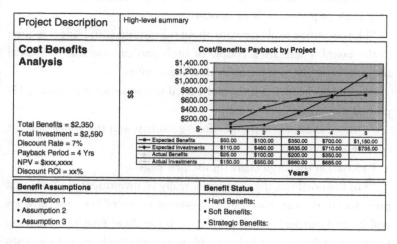

Figure 2.3   Cost–benefit analysis.

"So I don't have to implement everything the first year. That's why you asked me about how many projects the symphony can handle at one time."

"Precisely. You can create a similar portfolio roadmap and submit it to your board."

"Wow, I'll actually look like I know what I'm doing," I laughed.

"You'll be a pro by the time the season is over." Richardson put another paper in front of me.

"This is the cost-benefit analysis document or spreadsheet you can use for each project. It contains information like the total investment and how much it will cost. It can be used as a guesstimate of the total benefit that the organization can expect because of doing this project. It addresses any assumptions around the benefits as well as whether there are hard benefits like real dollars, soft benefits like intangible items, or strategic benefits. This will show the orchestra in a new light now that there are things like discount rates, payback periods, net present value, and discount ROI."

Richardson must have seen my eyes glaze over a bit.

"At this point, I don't think we need to go into those types of details for this list of projects," he continued. "But those are some things to consider. Do you have access to the online course I was telling you about?"

"Yeah, but I think I misplaced the link," I admitted.

Dr. Richardson quickly typed on his phone, and mine dinged, letting me know I had just received a text.

"I highly recommend you take time and look at that course. It teaches a lot of the same things I teach in my class, but you can do the lessons from the comfort of your home or office. Look it over, and it will walk you through and give you all the details around how to leverage all the components of a business cost-benefit analysis. It will show how each project should have a benefit-cost analysis along with the roadmap. This should give you what you need to present to the board regarding obtaining budget approval. I hope this helps."

"You have no idea," I replied. "This is exactly what I need. I promise I will be a better student than I was in your class."

"Jerry, you weren't a bad student. A distracted one, and I understand. Your focus was on music. I am very impressed you decided to expand your horizons a bit, and the symphony is lucky to have you."

"One last thing," said Dr. Richardson as he pushed a stack of stapled papers. "This is a great Harvard case study that will give you an even deeper understanding of portfolio management. I would suggest getting an account and downloading some of their other studies. They are excellent and much more eloquent than I am. I'll send you the link."

HARVARD CASE STUDY

MDCM, Inc. (B): Strategic IT Portfolio Management, https://hbr .org/product/mdcm-inc-b-strategic-it-portfolio-management/ KEL172?sku=KEL172-PDF-ENG

"Again, Dr. Richardson, I can't thank you enough."

"You keep buying me coffee, and you can have my ear for whatever you need. I can point you to what you need to do, but you have to put in the work."

As I drove home, I thought about all of the things Dr. Richardson had shared with me. As I got closer to home, my stomach twisted a little. Laura was still on my case about the new position. Maybe if I shared with her the progress I was making, she would change her mind. That was a big maybe.

IT'S ALL ABOUT THE BASS

"Did you get my text?" asked Laura as I barely got in the door.

"Yes, but I haven't had time to get to all those stores," I replied.

"What have you been doing all day?" Laura asked. "Your bass is over there, so I know you didn't have a rehearsal."

I looked at the floor. I was not looking forward to this conversation.

"I had to go to the symphony office, and then I met with Dr. Richardson."

"You what? You didn't take that job after you promised to turn it down?"

"I didn't promise anything," I replied. "You asked if I *could* turn it down. But I decided to give it a shot. Look, if I can't make it work, I'll quit."

"Then you need to quit because it's not working out," snapped Laura. "I need you to be able to run errands and do things with the kids."

I didn't want to remind her that she wasn't working, but I thought better of it.

"Listen, I can go out later and get those things. I wanted to be here when Corey got home."

"Never mind," she said as she grabbed the keys from my hand. "I'll handle it. I don't know why you insist on taking this job. You don't have any experience with it, and it doesn't pay enough for you to be away from home. I really hope for all of our sakes that you'll reconsider."

Linda came out of her room and said, "Mom, why are you doing this to Dad? I'm proud he is doing this new position. I think it's cool."

"You'll think it's really cool the next time you want to go to Betty's house, and your father is too busy to take you."

Laura didn't wait for a reply; she walked out of the house.

Linda gave me a big squeeze. "I'm sorry, Dad; I think Mom is being really unfair."

"Oh honey, don't worry about it. Everything is going to be just fine."

At that moment, the door burst open, and Corey came running into the house.

"Hey, Dad," he said as he dropped his backpack on the counter.

"Uh, the door, Corey," I said.

The doctors described Corey as having ADHD. I had to remind him constantly about closing doors.

"Oh yeah," he said without skipping a beat and ran to close the door.

"Hey, buddy, I have some good news I wanted to share with you."

"What?" Corey's face brightened.

"I heard from one of the other players today. They have a student bass that I can buy. I'll be able to pick it up next week."

"Really, Dad? Are you serious?"

"I am, but remember our deal. You need to practice every day. I'll invest in the instrument; you need to invest the time."

"I will . . . I promise."

I hadn't exactly cleared the bass thing with Laura. She didn't want the kids to follow in my footsteps as a musician. She felt they were destined to have careers in medicine or even technology. She didn't want them to struggle as I had as a professional musician. I disagreed. I loved my career, and just because I played in the orchestra didn't mean I couldn't also be good in business. I was determined to make my new job work and learn as much as I could from Dr. Richardson.

Dr. Richardson's Tips

- One of the key ways to organize a portfolio of projects is to organize them by what's known as a portfolio mix or categorization. This portfolio mix contains three buckets. One is transforming the business, another growing the business, and finally running the business. So think about your orchestra. You want to break the projects in the portfolio into three categories: transforming the symphony, growing the symphony, and running the symphony.
- For the portfolio, the roadmap is really an investment roadmap that provides short-, medium- and long-term views of how the projects will be laid out and which projects will get done first.

CHAPTER 3

SELECTING YOUR PROJECTS

"Portfolio Management Theory states that for any allocation of resources, an efficient set yields the greatest return for a given level of risk. While the right level of resources to allocate to projects cannot be known without considering further factors, what is clear is that once that level of investment is determined, then is there an optimal set of projects to implement for a given level of risk and investment?"

– Simon Moore

I hated sitting and waiting outside the board meeting. I was not privy to some of the other board business, and I was instructed to wait until I was called. I wanted to get it over with and move on with my day. I was extremely nervous. Maestro Fernando had not been much help with the budget. His attitude had been to just get it done. I felt like a failure in his presence – as if I had no clue what to do.

Sam made me feel better, but he was busy and not always available for questions. I probably would have quit if it weren't for Dr. Richard's help.

I looked at my watch again for the fifth time in ten minutes. My stomach gurgled. Did it mean I was hungry or anxious? Probably both.

The door finally opened, and Sam stepped out.

"Hey, Jerry. Thanks so much for waiting. We're breaking for lunch, so you can go pick up something. We're having our lunch brought in, so maybe come back in an hour, and we should be ready for you."

An hour? I wasn't sure eating was the best idea until my nerves were better, but I supposed a snack would be okay.

An hour later, I entered the room, and Maestro Fernando was holding court as he talked about his tour with a small orchestra in Tuscany a couple of summers ago. He was very charismatic, so people put up with his tirades and ego. There was no doubt that he was one of the most sought-after conductors in the world, but it didn't make me like him any better. It was one thing to see him at rehearsal for a few hours at a time, but now I had to endure his condemnation multiple times a week.

"Okay, everyone, Jerry is here. Let's get back to business," said Sam.

Fernando held up one finger, indicating he wasn't finished talking. I checked my PowerPoint on the projector while he continued to talk about wine and food. It seemed like the women on the board wanted to sleep with him, and the men wanted to be him. I just wanted to get started and get out of there.

Everyone eventually took their seats. Some of their eyes were droopy after large meals and a couple of lunchtime cocktails.

I went through my presentation, and it seemed that I had their attention most of the time. Fernando looked at his watch and never touched the packet I had provided with the budgets for the year.

At the end, I opened it up for questions, praying no one would have any.

"I have a question about your increase in pay for the musicians," said Dr. Ackerman. He had the largest, most successful eye care business in the area. "Do they really need that much more money?"

"What do you mean?" I was a little shocked.

"I mean, I know you all like playing, but is this really your job? It's more of a hobby. You know, a luxury. You can just write it off on your taxes."

I took a couple of deep breaths. I was usually a very calm and humble man. I could diffuse potential conflicts like a pro and was known for my level head. None of that mattered at the moment, as the first words that were trying to push their way out of my mouth would surely get me fired.

Hobby? Was he kidding?

I looked at Fernando, who had a grin on his face. What did he care? He was on a salary, and it was my job to get the best players to play. He wanted butts in seats and wasn't concerned about the cost.

Sam looked like he had swallowed a rock and it was stuck halfway down. He had warned me that not all of the board members appreciated what the symphony did. To them, it was a social event, and a few of them had a habit of ducking out of concerts halfway or never even came to the concerts. They were more concerned with looking their best at the preconcert dinner hosted by Maestro Fernando.

It was up to me to convince the board that the musicians deserved a raise. I was on my own, and I was going to have to earn my spot.

"Dr. Ackerman, how long have you known you wanted to be a doctor?"

"Well, I guess late in high school. I didn't really pick a specialty until later in my education."

"About how many hours a week does it take to prepare to go to the office or prepare for an eye surgery?"

"I don't know. I guess not many. I have been performing eye surgeries for years," said Dr. Ackerman, a little defensive.

"So you would say the surgeries you perform are routine? How many years did it take to learn a Lasik procedure?"

"That's a specialized procedure. It took about six months of training."

"Can you imagine having to learn a new procedure like that in about eight hours? Can you imagine having to learn a new one every few weeks?"

"Well, I . . ." Dr. Ackerman began.

"Can you imagine practicing your procedures four to five hours a day, every day?"

"That wouldn't . . ."

"I began playing the bass in the fifth grade. I began lessons in the sixth grade. I practiced thirty minutes to an hour every day through middle school. Once I got to high school, I was in three ensembles.

Between rehearsals and practice, I was playing about thirty hours a week. That didn't count hauling my bass in my parents' old station wagon."

Eyes around the table grew wide.

"I played in competitions and made it to the all-county and then the all-state orchestra. I was able to secure a scholarship to a music school. I was playing for hours every day, in addition to my regular classes and my music classes. I had three ensembles, a quartet, a masterclass, and individual lessons with my bass teacher. Once I graduated college, I played gigs every weekend, practiced every day, and had rehearsals four days a week. The cost of my instrument is $25,000. That doesn't take into account stands, a case, music, rosin, bow, and strings. The upkeep is in the thousands every year. So I want to ask you, Dr. Ackerman, does that sound like a hobby to you?"

Silence.

I was terrified. Where had that all bubbled up from? It was all true, but I was wielding that truth like a weapon. I looked around the room, and no one would meet my eyes except Maestro Fernando. He winked. I wasn't assured by his affirming look.

Dr. Ackerman scribbled some notes. He looked up.

"That was quite the speech."

"I'm sor . . ." I began

"And you are right. Everyone around this table has a love for music, but we are professionals and business owners. I myself played some piano as a child, but I had no talent for it, and I hated practicing. When we attend your concerts, you make the music sound so effortless to play, but I suppose that is the point. When I walk into a room, people have confidence in what I do, and they pay for my experience. I understand where you're coming from. While I am in support of your raise, we now have to figure out how to give it to you."

"I have created a projection over the next few years for a gradual increase. The good thing is we won't see an increase in the number of personnel, so those numbers are steady. I based them on the average number of concerts the last three years."

"You have asked for a number of new items for the budget," Dr. Ackerman continued. "I am not sure the board can approve all of them this year, but we could set some aside for the next few years. Can you send us a proposal of what you think are must-haves along with a list of things that would be nice for the symphony to have?"

"I can do that," I replied, making my own notes.

"Excellent job," said Sam. His jovial smile returned to his face. "It would be nice to have that early next week, if possible."

I left the meeting with mixed feelings. I was glad it was over, and it didn't go nearly as badly as my disaster fantasy had led me to believe. No one threw things at me or called me a fraud, so I could make a tick in the win box there.

Now I had to figure out how to make all these projects work. Dr. Richardson reminded me that I needed to take it one project at a time. I had all the groundwork done; now I had to put it in one concise report. Then the fun part would begin – putting all the pieces together and executing the plans.

★ ★ ★

"Well? Do you still have a job?" asked Laura before I barely got in the door.

"Yes, as a matter of fact, it went well," I replied.

I was disheartened to see the disappointment on her face.

"Well, I hope you can manage your time. I still think it's a bad idea. You don't have time for us anymore."

That was an untrue statement since I was taking the kids all around town after school, but I didn't want to argue.

I heard the scrapings of Corey practicing his bass. It was really hard for me not to run into the room and show him the proper posture and how to hold the bow, but he would be starting lessons next week. I preferred to have the teacher handle those things and to wait for Corey to ask me questions.

"Does that sound get better?" asked Laura.

"Yes, he just started. It takes time," I said.

"Well, I don't think my nerves can handle it today, so I need to go out. Can you pick up Linda?"

"Where is she?"

"Where is she all the time? Sally's."

"I don't think it is a good idea for her to be over there all the time," I replied. Linda was becoming more independent, and while I appreciated her spending time with friends, her grades weren't fantastic.

"You get to tell her," Laura replied.

I sat down at my computer to check my emails and noticed that my inbox was empty. That seemed odd, and so I looked in my spam folder. Just the usual outdated warranty notices. When I opened the trash folder, I was shocked. Emails for the past week were stacked there, all unseen and unanswered.

"Laura? Do you know what happened to my email?"

She entered my office with a strange look on her face. "What do you mean?"

"I mean that all my messages are in my trash file. Do you know anything about that?"

Her nostrils flared, and she crossed her arms. She remained mute.

"You do know something. . . ." Shock and horror filled my chest. "Did you do this?"

"Yes, yes okay . . . it was me," spat Laura. "I was using the computer to create fliers for the upcoming volunteer banquet that I agreed to host this year. While I worked on it, I noticed all the emails that would of course grab your utmost attention. I . . . I don't know why, but since you won't listen to me about this job quest of yours, I figured if you didn't answer your emails, they would fire you and then you'd have to follow my advice."

"Are you kidding me right now?" I was fuming.

"Jerry, you need to be here more. Why don't you just give lessons or teach at the school like other musicians? We need the money, but this is just crazy."

"This is a good job, Laura. It could help me with skills that will help me grow as a businessperson. Trying to live on a gig income is hard. Today I had to convince a member of the board that being a musician wasn't a hobby. I don't make near what he does as a doctor, so I could see it from his perspective. I can always make money as a musician, but I have to fight for every penny. This position is good for me as I hone my skills in project management. I can open new doors to a new career."

Laura's hands were on her hips now. "It's all about you. What about me and my needs?"

"I am listening . . . let me know what you need." I genuinely wanted to provide Laura with what she wanted. It was important to me.

"Oh, just forget it," she said as she turned back to the door. "You just don't understand."

Before I could say anything further, she was gone.

I turned back to my computer and immediately changed all my passwords. I knew this argument wasn't over, but I had work to do. Thirty-two emails weren't going to answer themselves.

★ ★ ★

The next day, Dr. Richardson and I sat at our usual table.

"I can't wait to hear Mahler's Fourth this weekend," he said.

"Yeah, it's quite a bear, and Fernando is sweating and swearing more than usual."

"You have quite the lineup for your final concert in a couple of weeks. Beethoven's Ninth with the choral society should be outstanding," commented Dr. Richardson.

"If I make it that long. This project management can be overwhelming," I admitted.

"Tell me about your board meeting. In your email, you said you thought it went well."

I told him about the positive reception I had but downplayed my speech about it not being just a hobby. He sipped his coffee and nodded, never interrupting.

"I have to provide them an itemized list of projects we need to get done right away and those things that can wait," I finished.

As usual, Dr. Richardson came prepared and handed me a small stack of papers.

"You had to rush to get your initial budget to the board; now I'd like to step back a little to make sure you understand portfolio management theory and what your role will be. I believe you'll feel a bit more at ease once you understand the process a bit more," Dr. Richardson explained.

"Anything will help; I'm all ears and ready to take notes," I replied.

"Great! Portfolio management theory is about identifying an optimal set of projects or work that is going to be undertaken, considering the limited resources and allocating those resources, and synchronizing the work so that no one is being a bottleneck with the activities that are going on and that you're also reducing the risk while at the same time maximizing the investment or the return investment that you're trying to accomplish."

"That sounds complicated," I admitted.

"Actually, you do this all the time when you go to the grocery store. You have a budget and know that you have to buy food for a week or two for your family. You know you can't go down the middle of the aisles and just get cookies and crackers and juice and things that are not going to give us the nutrition that our bodies need."

"Tell that to my kids," I chuckled.

"I bet. Because of your budget, you have to select the most efficient set or the right number of items that are going to give you the greatest return. You have to reduce the risk of eating too much sugar and all the things that can give you diabetes and other kinds of health difficulties. But at the same time, you want to purchase something that's going to give you the greatest return for the budget that you have."

"I get what you're saying."

"That is what project portfolio management and portfolio theory are all about. It's selecting that optimal set of projects, reducing risks, and maximizing your return. Your portfolio is a component collection of projects, programs, sub-portfolios, and operational work that is managed as a group to achieve a strategic objective. You following me so far?"

"Yes, I had read some of that in the materials you gave me and the online course you suggested, but this has clarified it for me a lot."

"Great, then let's talk about your role as the project manager. Portfolio management is a set of skills and/or capabilities that enables an organization, or a team within an organization, to analyze, select, and manage a collection of project investments that are aligned with the company's goals and objectives. And that's within a data-driven decision-making framework. And that's important because now you're making decisions based on data and not based on someone who screams the loudest or has bigger opinions or has a stronger walking stick. But it's based on data to make sure that the investments are all aligned to where the symphony is going."

I thought about Dr. Ackerman and how badly I had handled my interaction with him. I wish I could have handled it from a position of understanding that I needed to demonstrate why increasing the symphony musician's salary would benefit the overall organization.

"Portfolio management coordinates the acceptance, approval, postponement, rejection, and/or cancellation of a project that will not realize the proposal benefits or the symphony's strategic outcomes."

"Can you explain that a bit further?" I asked.

"It's a set of skills, and it's also a set of governance processes around allowing projects to start, to be put on hold, or to be terminated or canceled because they're not going to deliver what they promise. They want to know that what you're proposing is going to work in the way you say, or they might pull the plug on it. Organizations like the symphony are not in the habit of spending good money after bad. They seek to use their resources optimally."

"So that's why they want me to prioritize the projects for this year and subsequent years. They need my help to tell them what is essential right now and what can wait a bit."

"Exactly," said Dr. Richardson. "Let me explain your role as the portfolio manager a little further. This is really important because you need to understand what the symphony board is expecting of you. You need to be oriented toward the symphony's strategic goals. It's not just about delivering a project on time and on budget. It's about accomplishing the symphony's strategic goals. You will be called upon to help out with metrics, not just the metrics that you're working on of scope, schedule, and cost, but also managing risk on a project and the symphony as well. In addition, you're being called upon to work with other staff in the symphony. They are managing a project or a part of a project, but as the portfolio manager, you'll be looking over all the projects."

"That sounds like a lot of work and a huge responsibility," I said. "Maybe my wife was right."

"Nonsense. Once you have processes in place, it will be much easier to manage. You will then just have to make sure the projects are on track and report back to the board. You have to consider the organization's culture. Think about how the delivery of your portfolio is going to impact the organization's culture and whether everyone is positioned to absorb all of these changes that we're planning on rolling out. This is why I cautioned not to get too crazy with changes all at once. Introduce big change over time."

"I'll definitely take your advice on that," I replied.

"Finally, one of the greatest focuses for you as a portfolio manager is that you have to change your mindset and focus on creating value at the much larger level within the organization. It's not just about getting musicians in seats; it is about how you can help improve the symphony overall. Not just to please the board members but to impress the audience. I have seen more empty seats in the past couple of years in the audience, so you'll be in a prime position to help them turn that around."

Dr. Richardson pointed at some of the papers.

"I've included a link to the Vermont Teddy Bear HBR Case study (https://store.hbr.org/product/peak-experiences-and-strategic-it-alignment-at-vermont-teddy-bear/JIT031). It covers the important principles of project portfolio management and places you in the shoes of the CIO, who's challenged with aligning the IT strategy with the corporate business goals or managing severe resource constraints and competitive forces. I know it isn't about a symphony, but these strategies work in any type of company. So by reading this case study, you kind of get into the mind of a CIO and portfolio managers and what they really go through in real-world situations."

Dr. Richard pointed at a graphic. (See Figure 3.1.)

"This high-level roadmap shows how major projects are connected to broad strategic goals. This is meant to capture initiatives linked to major business goals, not as a repository of all tactical project work. You can use this roadmap to show the board the broad horizon of the projects that you intend to implement and linkages to objectives."

"Okay, this makes sense," I said.

"I'm going to email you a tool you can use to design initiatives that will enable you and those you partner with to deliver needed

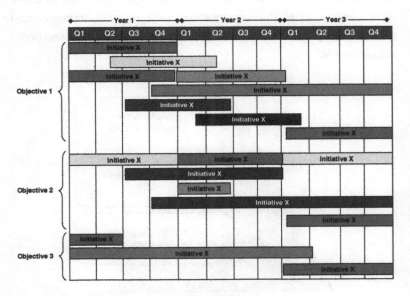

Figure 3.1   Three-year portfolio roadmap.

capabilities for the symphony. You already have your list of the initiative this year, and I believe you have prioritized them. You can now use this tool to map out a multi-year roadmap for your projects by strategic objective."

(Fidelity Investments, https://www.eaec.executiveboard.com/Members/Events/EventReplayAbstract.aspx?cid=100047046. See also Aligning the Portfolio with Business Strategy - The Gillette Approach   https://www.eaec.executiveboard.com/Members/Events/EventReplayAbstract.aspx?cid=100064512&fs=1&q=Gillette&program=&ds=1)

"So how do I figure out what things have the most weight? How do I figure out what I need to get done this year?"

Dr. Richardson pointed at another paper in the stack. (See Figure 3.2.)

"Most companies break up their investments in three areas. As you can see, the projects that help run the business get the most resources, then growing the business and then finally transforming the business," he explained. "That's where I would begin. You need to know what's important to the organization, come up with strategies, and then fit your projects into that matrix. That's what I believe the board is looking for."

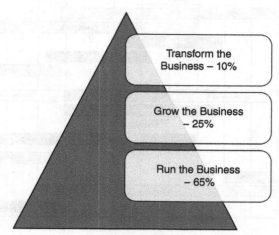

Figure 3.2   Categorizing investment types.

I thanked Dr. Richardson for all his help. I had a lot to think about, but I felt like I understood my role way more after he clarified it. I was ready to roll up my sleeves and start digging in.

Dr. Richardson's Tips

- Portfolio management and theory are about identifying an optimal set of projects or work that is going to be undertaken, considering the limited resources, allocating resources, and synchronizing the work so that no one is being a bottleneck with the activities that are going on, and that you're also reducing the risk while at the same time maximizing the investment or the return investment that you're trying to accomplish.
- Portfolio management is a set of skills and/or capabilities that enables an organization, or a team within an organization, to analyze, select, and manage a collection of project investments that are aligned with the company's goals and objectives.
- The high-level roadmap shows how major projects are connected to broad strategic goals. This is meant to capture initiatives linked to major business goals, not as a repository of all tactical project work. You can use this roadmap to show the board the broad horizon of the projects that you intend to implement and linkages to objectives.

CHAPTER 4

CHOOSING YOUR PORTFOLIO PROCESSES

I wanted to bang my head on my desk. The roster database was a mess: missing addresses, phone numbers that needed updating, old email addresses that bounced. The list went on. I needed to figure out who would be returning and get the contracts signed.

I did decide that I could speed up the process by creating a PDF document that would accept electronic signatures. That way I wouldn't have to wait for contracts in the mail. My challenge was getting updated emails and getting musicians to buy in. Those who weren't as tech-savvy were resistant, even though, to me, the process seemed simple. I needed to call those from whom I could not get a contract back right away, and at least get a verbal commitment that they would be returning.

I was kicking myself that I hadn't started the process sooner. I could have talked to the musicians and gotten some contracts signed at the last concert. The problem was that I had to wait for the final raise amounts and structure my rates.

First-chair players received more money than the rest of their section. Those who played more than one instrument, such as the flute/piccolo player, also got a higher rate. It seemed like a simple process, but it wasn't. Mileage was also a factor. If someone lived more than 50 miles away, they got a pay bump to cover gas. Some of the specialty instruments, like the bass clarinet, only played a couple of concerts per season but often demanded higher pay.

I decided to put it all in a spreadsheet, which was a better system than torn sheets of notebook paper and a stack of old contracts. I had to take time and streamline the entire system. Only once it was in a spreadsheet could I begin to see the gaps we needed to fill for the next season.

"Hey, Susan, this is Jerry from the symphony," I said on the phone. "Listen, I'm calling about next season. I need a harp for at least four of the concerts."

"What are the dates?" asked Susan.

I rattled off the dates of the rehearsals and performances.

"I will have a conflict with the December date. I'm playing in Roanoke," she replied.

That wasn't good news. That was a big concert with the choir, and there was a big part for the harp.

"Is there anyone you can recommend?" I asked. I didn't have any harp subs on my list.

"Perhaps Sandra can do it, but that's a bad time of year. We usually book Christmastime concerts a year in advance."

That was something to note, but the schedule hadn't been decided until March, so I couldn't have booked people sooner.

"Do you by chance have her number?" I asked.

Susan gave it to me.

"Do you mind if I email you the contract? You don't have to mail it; you can just sign it online," I said. I held my breath.

"Oh, that sounds wonderful," she said. "Is that new this year?"

"Yes, I'm trying it out. I've had mixed reviews," I admitted.

"Well, you're in charge of the musicians now," she replied. "You just need to tell them that is the new policy. They might resist, but they'll figure it out. They don't want to be without work."

"Thanks," I said, and we ended the call.

I moved on to my next call. "Sandra," I said timidly. I hated cold calls. "This is Jerry from the symphony. I got your number from Susan Or.

She said you might be able to play a concert we have in December."
I gave her the dates.

"I can do all of those dates except the second rehearsal. I have a church gig on that night. Will that work?"

I had a decision to make. Harps were not easy to find, and Susan had told me that December was particularly bad. I could continue to try to find someone, but I had no list to go on. I would have to continue to ask other musicians, and I didn't think that was the best use of my time.

"Do you mind if I call you back?" I asked.

"No, that's fine. Talk to you soon," said Sandra.

The next call I dreaded.

"Maestro Fernando, this is Jerry," I began. "I am having difficulty finding a harpist who can do all of the dates for the December concert. I have one person, but she can't do the second rehearsal."

"Is she any good?" asked Fernando.

"Well . . . I don't know. Susan Or recommended her, so I assume that she is," I stuttered.

"But you don't personally know?" he asked.

"Well, no."

"Who else did you call?" asked Fernando.

My stomach was twisting.

"I . . . I don't have any sub-harp players on the list I was given," I murmured. "Susan said most harp players book out a year in advance."

"Come on, Jerry. You have to do better than this," spat Fernando. "See if you can find a sub for that rehearsal. That person better be good . . . real good, because that is a difficult piece."

I had to commit and stand by it.

"I trust Susan, and Sandra, the woman I called, was familiar with the piece and had played it before."

"You need to build a solid sub-list this year, Jerry. I am counting on you for that. Maybe we can pick some up during auditions in a couple of weeks."

"Yes, about that," I said. Even though I knew he would resist it, I had to remind him of my idea and now was as good a time as any. "As I mentioned to you before, I want to change auditions to blind auditions."

"Why?" snapped Fernando.

"Some of the musicians have complained and feel the process isn't fair. And many other symphonies have adopted blind auditions."

"We aren't other symphonies," Fernando barked back.

"I understand. But they are right. You have tasked me with filling the seats with the best musicians. This is a great way to do that because you would be basing your decision on how they play, rather than what they look like or who they are."

There was a long pause on the other side, and I was afraid he had hung up on me.

"We can try it out this year. But I still get the last say on who I pick. Even if the committee likes one player and I don't, I make the final call, capeesh?"

"Yes, Maestro."

"Is there anything else? I am busy scoring today."

"Nope, that was it. Thank you."

I hung up the phone quickly and felt like I might throw up.

★ ★ ★

"Jerry," yelled Laura across the house. "I need my big suitcase."

I had been working for hours calling and emailing people. I supposed looking through closets would break the monotony a bit.

"I'll look up here," I yelled back.

I began going through the closets and came up with nothing. The last one was a utility closet off the laundry room. I opened it, and I gasped.

"Laura," I yelled out the door, "I need you to come upstairs a minute."

While I waited, I began opening boxes. A lot of boxes. They were filled with clothes, gadgets, and all manner of kitchen appliances. Stamped on each box was a familiar smile logo.

"Yes?" said Laura with her hands on her hips.

"Laura, can you explain this . . . all this? Most of this stuff hasn't even been opened."

"Jerry, you know I normally buy the kids' Christmas gifts early, especially when I find bargains. Also, I purchased some items for the volunteer banquet, along with a few new outfits for my trip," said Laura.

"And . . . and . . . how did you purchase all this stuff?" I asked.

"I used our credit and debit cards, of course," she replied simply.

"Laura . . . we can't afford all this," I said. "You are now going on a weekend in Vegas with your friends."

"It's a bachelorette weekend for Tiana and I needed some new clothes."

"Yeah, I know," I replied.

"And you already said it wasn't going to be a problem."

"Yeah, but that was because I thought we both understood our budget and the spending would be reasonable. Instead, you've bought a great deal of things and hidden it all without one word about the total costs. I don't know if any future purchases or trips can be made," I replied.

"I wasn't hiding it. It's in plain sight. If you were home more often and helped out with the laundry, you would have seen it and it wouldn't be an issue," replied Laura.

"Are you kidding me right now?"

"You have that new job as personnel manager, and so I didn't think it would matter."

"I'm not a millionaire all of a sudden. Sure, we have a better, more stable income, but that doesn't mean we won a lottery. We have to send some of this back."

"Hmph," pouted Laura. "Well, I definitely need the clothing for this weekend. If you insist the other stuff goes back, then you can do all the returns."

"Me? When am I going to have time to do all of that? I'm playing this weekend, and I have to finish finding musicians."

"Well, I can't. I'm not going to be here. Oh, you need to add to your list that you need to talk to Linda. I found a note from the school in her backpack. Apparently, her grades are slipping, and we need to talk to the teacher."

I was punched in the gut. Linda had always been a straight-A student. But lately she had been moodier and was staying at her friend's house a lot.

"Where is she?" I asked.

"Where do you think?"

"She needs to stay home this weekend," I said.

"That's on you; I won't be here. I've already spoken with her about her grades and spending so much time visiting her friend. She isn't listening to me."

"Okay, then I'll talk to her about her grades and tell her that she can't stay at her friend's house this weekend."

Laura reached under the last pile of boxes and pulled out her suitcase.

"Great. I found my suitcase," she said, as she left the room.

★ ★ ★

Linda sat across the table. Her hot chocolate was becoming cold.

"Are you going to say anything?" I asked.

"What do you want me to say? I'm grounded. I get it. It's like I'm a toddler or something," Linda snapped.

"No one said you were a toddler."

"Yeah, then why do I have cocoa in front of me? That is not exactly a drink for a teen."

"I thought you loved hot chocolate," I replied.

"Yeah, when I was eight."

This wasn't going well, and we were losing focus fast.

"I wanted to talk to you about your grades. We found a note that said you were making Ds and even failing a couple of classes."

"You didn't find anything," Linda retorted. "Mom was snooping in my stuff, like she always does. Maybe I should start leaving an empty beer can or a pill bottle."

"Linda! Come on, let's be reasonable," I said.

"Reasonable? Even police need a warrant to perform a search. Besides, why should you care? You never cared what I did before."

That hurt. A lot. I loved my family, and they came before anything. I cared more about them than they could ever fathom.

"I do care," I replied. "That's why I wanted to talk to you. To find out what's going on. You were always a great student, and this is so unlike you."

"Why should I care about an education? Mom has a degree. She just sits at home all day and spends your money. Seems like a great job with benefits."

Another stab.

"This isn't about your mom," I said, trying to keep focus. "This is about you."

"Of course it's about Mom and you." Tears began running down her face. "You guys are fighting all the time, and no one seems to care if I'm even here anymore, so why should I care about school?"

I walked over to the other side of the table to hug Linda. At first she resisted, and then the sobbing began and she fell into my embrace.

"Oh, honey, I am so sorry. Of course, you matter. And yes, your mom and I are running through a rough patch right now."

"A rough patch? You know Mom has been looking up divorce laws online. She wants to know how much money she should expect for alimony."

The third stab hurt the worst, and it was a direct hit to my heart.

"How do you know that?" I asked.

"Mom isn't the only snoop. I looked at her browser history. She doesn't do a very good job at hiding what she's doing."

"You know it isn't right to spy on your mom."

"And it isn't right how she's treating you, Dad. And you just sit by and let her do it." More tears welled up in her eyes.

"Honey, I will talk to your mom. You guys mean the world to me, and this is a wake-up call. Maybe Mom and I need to go to counseling."

"Really?" said Linda in a surprised tone. "Do you think she'll go?"

"That's for me to worry about. I can't ignore the grades, so you need to be grounded for the weekend, and I expect a better report starting next week. Do you understand?"

I was trying to be the tough dad, but at the moment it felt like pushing a boulder uphill. I worried every second that the boulder would roll back and crush me.

"Yes, Dad. I've been so worried that you and Mom were breaking up. That's why I've been away so much. I just can't deal with it."

"Then your mom and I need to fix it. Besides, I'd like to have you around. We can cook together and maybe watch some movies with your brother."

"I get to pick the movies," Linda insisted.

"Okay, but they have to be appropriate for your brother."

"Deal," replied Linda with a smile I hadn't seen in months. "Oh, and Dad. Hot chocolate . . . really?"

"I thought you loved it. What do you like to drink now?"

"I don't know, a vodka martini, shaken, not stirred."

"Not on your life, Linda Bond."

We both broke up with laughter.

* * *

"How was your week?" asked Dr. Richardson.

"Don't ask," I replied with a weak chuckle. We were at our regular spot, and it was unusually empty. There was a game going on, and this was a college hangout, so it made sense.

"Did you get your roster filled?"

"Yes and no. I'm still struggling to find musicians. We have auditions coming up, and we've put up announcements everywhere, so I hope we have a good turnout."

"Oh, how did Fernando take the news about your new way of doing auditions?" Dr. Richardson asked.

"Poorly, but he will allow it."

"Do you believe this new way of doing things is good for the orchestra?"

"Yes, I do. We need the best musicians, and we don't need to play favorites or pick a player because of how they look. Doing blind auditions not only helps put the best musicians in the right seats, but it also promotes more inclusion."

"Creating a new project isn't always easy," replied Dr. Richardson. "You've done an excellent job of identifying a need for your symphony. It's not always easy to get buy-in. That takes time. How will you know your idea is a success?"

"Well, we should sound better, and I hope the responses of the audience reflect that."

"That's a key point – eliciting and paying attention to the feedback of your customers, and in this case your audience. Do you have a way to capture those responses?"

"We usually send out a survey at the end of the year."

"Does that seem often enough?" Dr. Richardson asked.

"Perhaps not," I mused. "I'll have to think about that."

Dr. Richardson had another stack of papers. I had been taking the papers home and putting them in a growing notebook. The instruction was invaluable, and after reviewing what he said and the resources he had given me and reading the articles, I was beginning to become more confident with the project management process.

I looked at the first page as Dr. Richardson continued to speak. (See Figure 4.1.)

"We're going to dive a little deeper now in the process, so stop me if I'm going too fast."

I had my notebook and pen ready. "Gotcha."

"As you can see from the chart, which I've created based on the Standard for Portfolio Management from the Project Management Institute, there are five knowledge areas, which are strategic management, governance, performance management, communication management, and risk management. There are also three process types,

Knowledge Area	Defining Process Group	Aligning Process Group	Authoring and Controlling Process Group
Portfolio Strategic Management	4.1 Develop Portfolio Strategic Plan 4.2 Develop Portfolio Charter 4.3 Define Portfolio Roadmap	4.4 Manage Strategic Change	
Portfolio Governance	5.1 Develop Portfolio Management Plan 5.2 Define Portfolio	5.3 Optimize Portfolio	5.4 Authorize Portfolio 5.5 Provide Portfolio Oversight
Portfolio Performance Management	6.1 Develop Portfolio Performance Management Plan	6.2 Manage Supply and Demand 6.3 Manage Portfolio Value	
Portfolio Communication Management	7.1 Develop Portfolio Communication Management Plan	7.2 Manage Portfolio Information	
Portfolio Risk Management	8.1 Develop Portfolio Risk Management Plan	8.2 Manage Portfolio Risk	

Figure 4.1 Portfolio management process group.

which are defining processes, aligning processes, and authoring and controlling processes. The sixteen processes provide a framework for the core elements that make up project portfolio management.

"And as you can see from the chart, going from left to right, we have the names of the processes in the process groups. Then we have the three process types, and you can see that under the defining process, which is kind of like your planning area. You have more processes there for each of those areas, especially in the first section there for developing a portfolio strategic plan, developing the portfolio charter, and defining their portfolio roadmap."

"Okay, I follow," I responded.

"Great. And then you go into the aligning processes. And this is all about calibration and executing on the portfolio. And then the authoring and controlling processes. These are all about giving authority to start components of a portfolio, which is launching a project or launching a program or approving additional operational work, and then providing reports and oversight of the overall portfolio. Think about how that relates to your auditions."

"Okay, that makes sense."

"So let's talk about strategic planning and the portfolio. Strategic planning sets the context within which the portfolio management operates by addressing the following four questions. Are the programs and projects in our portfolio necessary in the context of our strategic objectives? In the case of the auditions, you have clearly demonstrated that they are. Think about: Is your portfolio, together with your operational work, sufficient to achieve the strategic objectives? Is the overall level of risk acceptable, and is the portfolio of initiatives achievable? And is the portfolio affordable, and if not, which initiatives should be killed or rescheduled?"

"So if my plan for the auditions doesn't work or is a disaster, I should be ready to pull the plug and move on."

"Yes, but you need to allow it the space to work. Just because one or two people don't like your new idea doesn't mean it's a bad one. So let me add a little context to this with some background. I worked for an international law firm where I implemented a portfolio management solution, and initially when they brought me in, I had to kind of shore up the project management processes because they really didn't have a lot of framework and structure around their projects. I went through and laid out all the things we needed to do to have great project management and started teaching the project managers through lunch-and-learns, not unlike what we're doing here."

"Oh, so there is a method to your madness," I joked.

"Of course! Well, once we started really being able to execute a lot of projects, we had to then look at the portfolio because initially they were using a lot of spreadsheets. We began to leverage the portfolio tool, and as we were going through the process, it became clear that we needed to go through this exercise of working with the CIO and the managing partners of the law firm to look at the strategic plan and then aligning projects into certain categories and areas and also understanding our portfolio mix. Basically, we're mapping apples to apples and oranges to oranges and bananas to bananas when we are deciding what's going to be in the portfolio and what's not going to be in the portfolio."

"So I need to begin matching up projects and putting them together in categories."

"Precisely. Why reinvent the wheel? Much of what you're doing overlaps and so if you have projects that are together, you can kill many birds with one stone. You can overlap your auditions with your new payroll system, and you can roll out your plans for getting music to the musicians by explaining your process up front."

"That's brilliant."

"It was an amazing exercise to watch this international law firm, which was in five countries and 14 offices, go from no processes to having these processes and being able to see the integration of the managing partners developing the strategic plan of where the law firm needed to be and the execution of that through the portfolio. We were able to close the gaps. I worked very closely with the enterprise architect within the group so that when he developed the current architecture and then the target architecture, that gap between them became the roadmap in which the portfolio led. It was an amazing exercise. I got a lot of great insights from it, and I wanted to pass that on to you as we talk about this concept of strategic planning and the portfolio, because they are totally integrated and intertwined.

"I've really been enjoying the articles that you recommended," I admitted. "They take a little time to get through, but they make total sense when I review our notes."

"I'm so glad to hear that. Once you have a strategic plan and a selection of portfolio components, projects, programs, and sub-portfolios that you're going to manage, you can get into operational strategy and the portfolio. Peter Drucker says management is doing things right; leadership is doing the right things. So strategic goals have to be defined before project selection. That's strategic planning. A clear set of strategic goals is critical to selecting and mapping projects that will create value and move the organization forward toward its desired capabilities to achieve its strategic goals and objectives. You've been doing an excellent job of that."

"You think so?" I asked.

"Absolutely. They picked the right person for the job. You are using your instincts and are doing a great job," replied Dr. Richardson.

"I feel lost a lot."

"Give yourself time. Value creation is primarily a result of one or two of those projects that generate the desired benefit needed to fulfill the targeted objective. And strategic alignment should produce an aligned outcome and greater efficiency within the organization. Once the portfolio is selected, you then have to look at the organizational strategy and how you get into the day-to-day operations of the organization. You have already begun that. Now start to focus on things along the lines we're talking about: maintaining the alignment, allocating financial resources, allocating the human resources, allocating material resources, and tracking the operational performance and the organization's performance, as well as managing the organizational risk. And think about the risk to the symphony at the organizational level, not just at the project level."

"I'm trying to do that, but I think I'm going to hit resistance," I replied.

"You will, and that is totally normal. But if you've done all the work, you won't get as much resistance as you think you will because they will see that these projects will improve not only the symphony but the entire organization."

Dr. Richardson pointed at another paper in my packet. (See Figure 4.2.)

"One of my favorite topics to teach is about the corpus callosum, which is a large bundle of fibers connecting the right and left hemispheres of the brain. Each hemisphere controls the movement of the opposite side of the body and can also specialize in performing specific cognitive and perceptual functions. It enables information to move between hemispheres and is therefore a very important integrative structure. Think of project portfolio management as the corpus callosum of your symphony. The same way the corpus callosum links the two halves of the brain to align your vision with your action, the portfolio management processes link an organization's vision, mission, and strategic objective with the companies, agencies, and organization's actions."

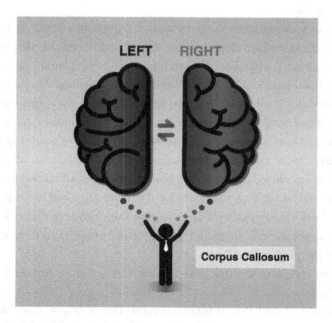

Figure 4.2   The corpus callosum for the business.

"Okay, I can visualize it."

"The corpus callosum allows for information to go back and forth between the halves. Have you ever seen someone who's really good at art or visual activities as well as mathematics? They have a well-integrated and robust corpus callosum, which means information goes back and forth between the two hemispheres. If someone's corpus callosum is damaged, they'll have a lot of challenges and issues and probably will be in a place where they can't take care of themselves because, while they might have a vision for what they think they want to do, they can't communicate with the other part of their brain to actually carry it out."

"That makes sense," I said.

"If we have a portfolio measure process that's working, then we can have a strategic plan that we visualize where we want the organization to go, and then we're able to work through project portfolio management to execute on that strategy. If we have a damaged project portfolio management process, like a damaged corpus callosum, then we may have a vision for where we want the organization to go, but we don't have the capability to actually deliver on that."

"I like that visual," I said.

"Remember that story about the Vermont Teddy Bear Company?"

"Yeah, sure."

"Let me tell you a little more. Bob was the CIO. His career path prepared him for the various challenges he would eventually face at Vermont Teddy Bear. During his career, he was a database administrator, a web developer, an enterprise content management specialist, a CRM admin, a business intelligence consultant, a software developer, and a supply chain management support member. And in his first year as CIO, he lost five of the twelve IT staff, and a few of them had institutional knowledge of the IT environment that had not been documented during their tenure. Bob needed to quickly develop an IT architectural document that captured the current IT environment and model of their IT infrastructure. If you were Bob, what processes would you put into place first? Just think about it; you don't have to answer me right now."

"Got it," I scratched down some notes.

"Well, that should keep you busy this week," commented Dr. Richardson.

"It should, and again I can't thank you enough."

"It's my pleasure. Keep up the great work!"

Dr. Richardson's Tips

- Strategic planning sets the context within which the portfolio management operates by addressing the following four questions:
  - Are the programs and projects in our portfolio necessary in the context of our strategic objectives?
  - Is your portfolio, together with your operational work, sufficient to achieve the strategic objectives?
  - Is the overall level of risk acceptable, and is the portfolio of initiatives achievable?
  - Is the portfolio affordable, and if not, which initiatives should be killed or rescheduled?"
- One of my favorite topics to teach is the corpus callosum, which is the part of the brain that connects the right and left hemispheres. Think of project portfolio management as the corpus callosum of your symphony. In the same way that the corpus callosum links the two halves of the brain to align your vision with your action, the portfolio management processes link an organization's vision, mission, and strategic objective with the companies, agencies, and organization's actions.

CHAPTER 5

CHOOSING YOUR STRATEGY

"RJ," I said frantically, looking through the symphony library for Beethoven's Third Symphony. "Where are all the string parts?"

As the music librarian, RJ was in charge of music parts for the symphony members. Some of the pieces the symphony played were ones they owned and were available in the library. Other pieces had to be rented, and when there was a new piece, he received the parts in the mail from the composers. He had to make sure each musician received their music in time to begin practicing their parts prior to the first rehearsal.

Two weeks was the standard, but in the past couple of years, parts were missing or were not handed out until the first rehearsal. I had witnessed Fernando throwing a baton at RJ when he realized that none of the cello section had their parts.

"Well, that's a piece we own, but the parts have gone missing through the years," he said. "Musicians don't return them after the concert, or they lose their part and I have to scramble to get them a copy."

This was a chaotic system that wasn't working. I had proposed a more digital approach, but it seemed to have landed on deaf ears.

"We need the parts to send to musicians to have for the audition packets. I'm not even going to mail them," I said. "I just need them to scan and then email them and have a few copies available at the symphony office if someone wants to pick them up."

RJ was flipping through torn envelopes and folders to look for the parts. He was one of the first-chair violins, and we had known each other a long time. We both answered to Sam, but I was in a new position as the personnel manager. RJ and I would need to create a system that worked for both of us.

"Did you get my email about scanning all the music and sending that to the musicians?" I asked.

"Yeah, I don't know . . ." RJ began. "A lot of the musicians don't have printers and aren't very tech-savvy."

"But it would save the symphony time and money," I said. "Mailing out music is becoming expensive, and emails are free. As you said, we're losing music, and I imagine that is costing us unnecessary funds to replace."

"I hear what you're saying, but we aren't there yet," said RJ as he continued to search for parts, some of which were barely stuck together with tape. "Besides, we aren't supposed to be copying music that way."

"We are copying parts anyway when they go missing. We can even print out parts for musicians at the first rehearsal rather than giving them the originals. I did read that as long as we actually have the originals, we can copy them for the musicians. We just have to destroy the copies. Besides, there is nothing preventing the musicians from making copies themselves."

"It seems like a lot of extra work," replied RJ. I was hoping he realized the irony in his statement since digging and replacing music seemed a lot more time-consuming. "I have another job, and that would be tough for me to do."

"I don't mind making copies," I said.

"Even so, it doesn't seem like the musicians will like it. They're used to having their parts mailed out, or if they're lucky, I give them their parts for the next concert at a performance."

I thought about it for a moment. He was right in some ways. I thought it was a great idea, but I wasn't sure everyone in the symphony felt that way. It would help save money and time, but it was also important for the players to have input.

We finished finding the parts, and I took them to the scanner so I could email them out for those auditioning. It was a week out, which was kind of short notice, but at least we had the list of the audition music posted and emailed. Sending the parts was a benefit to the musicians, so they wouldn't have to search or even buy the parts for their audition.

As the light of the scanner moved back and forth, I thought of the perfect person to talk to in order to get insight into the symphony – Cindy Wittaker, the head of the orchestral committee. I decided to call her right away.

CALL TO CINDY

"Hey, Cindy," I said when she answered the phone.

"Oh hey, Jerry, great to hear from you," she answered. "How is your new position?"

"Great. It is actually the reason I called you. Do you have a minute?"

"Sure."

"I spoke to RJ today about the issue of getting parts to musicians and then getting them back. Some of the musicians aren't getting their parts on time; they might get lost in the mail, or for all sorts of reasons. Losing parts and even mailing them is costing the symphony a lot of money. I've asked the board for raises, and they're on board, but I also promised I would find ways to cut costs and modernize some of our processes."

"Sounds great. I agree. I hate getting my parts late, mostly because if I'm not prepared, Maestro knows it."

"I agree. So my solution is to scan all the parts, email them to musicians, and then have copies available on the stands for the first rehearsal. That way, musicians don't have to have the originals, and they can have the parts on time."

"What did RJ say?" asked Cindy.

"Well . . . he felt like it would be extra work and that the musicians wouldn't want it," I replied.

"I, for one, would appreciate it, but I can understand his point. He has some musicians who might be tech adverse, mostly because they don't understand it."

"Listen, I don't mind if we send out a couple of parts if a few people are against doing it by email," I replied. "But it would really save time and resources to have the majority receive them by email, or we can even have them on a secured server for them to download."

"Is that legal?" asked Cindy.

"I plan to talk to Sam about it more, to be sure," I replied. "In the meantime, since you're the head of the orchestral committee, do you think you could survey the musicians and get their feel for it before we get into this any deeper?"

"I think that's an excellent idea. The committee works this week. We can send out emails and call people to get their take, and then I can give you the results the following week?"

"That would be perfect," I replied.

After hanging up the phone, I realized it was time to go home, and my stomach turned a bit. Things weren't great, and I really wasn't looking forward to it. All I could do was to keep my chin up and hope for the best.

HOME IS WHERE THE HEART ISN'T

When I walked in the door, Laura was standing in the kitchen with her hands on her hips.

"You're late," she said.

I looked at my watch. It was 5:30.

"Late for what?" I asked. "This is the usual time I get home."

"Well, I have plans tonight, and I need to leave."

"Plans? What plans?" I asked.

"I told you last week, my girlfriends and I were going on a girls' night out."

I noticed she was dressed in an eye-catching new dress, along with matching accessories. It was definitely not an outfit I had seen before.

"You mentioned something about it, but you never said it was for sure or when it was," I replied.

"Well, I did tell you, and I have to leave in five minutes." she pouted.

"Hey, Dad!" said Corey. "Am I still going to my lesson at six?"

Dang. It was Thursday. Laura usually took him on Thursdays, but I knew this was not the time to argue. Actually, I wasn't sure any time was a good time to argue. Laura had moved from passive-aggressive to aggressive-aggressive a lot lately, and so I was at a loss for what to do.

"Sure, buddy, load up your bass, and I'll be right there," I said.

Once Corey left the room, I asked. "Where's Linda? And have they had anything to eat?"

"No, I didn't have time to make anything. And as for Linda, I think she's in her room. I need to get going. You don't have me blocked in, do you?" asked Laura.

"No, but can we have some time to talk this weekend?" I asked.

"About what?"

"Well, things have been a bit strained between us for a while and it seems to be getting worse. I think we need to talk about it," I replied.

"Things are strained because you're never around. I have a life too, you know. I have to do everything for the kids while you do this new job thing."

"Can we agree to talk about it later?" I answered.

"Sure, we can talk later," Laura said as she grabbed her keys and purse and left for the evening.

I ran up the stairs to see Linda before I took off with Corey. I knocked on her door.

"Linda?" I asked. "Can I talk to you quickly?"

"Yeah," said a small voice.

I was shocked to see Linda on her bed, hugging her pillow and crying.

"Oh, honey, what's the matter?" I asked.

Her eyes were wide, and she looked at me with an odd expression.

"You . . . you aren't mad?" she stuttered.

"Mad? About what?"

"Mom didn't tell you?"

I sat down at the foot of her bed. "Tell me what?"

"I got cut from the squad," she said and began sobbing.

"You did what?" I handed her a box of tissues from her dresser.

"Well . . . I missed a couple of practices . . . but it was more about . . . my grades."

"Your grades? I thought you were working on them?"

"I have been, but I couldn't get my GPA up before the end of midterms, and now I can't be on the team. Ms. Hassleback called Mom about it today. She was really mad and yelled at me. She blames you, and I told her it wasn't your fault. That you were helping me get my grades up, and that only made her madder. I thought you'd be mad too."

"I know you've been working hard since we had that talk. Maybe I can call Ms. Hassleback tomorrow and see what can be done. I have to take Corey to his lesson. You want to come with us, and then we can get Chinese afterward?"

Linda jumped up and almost tackled me with her hug.

"I'd love that," she said. "Thank you, Dad!"

★ ★ ★

As I drove to meet with Dr. Richardson, I thought a lot about my life. Things were going better in my new position, and I was learning a lot about project management, and for that I felt blessed. But my personal life was a mess. Maybe I needed to look at my home life as a project.

"Hey, Jerry," said Dr. Richardson as he held out his hand. "A pleasure as always!"

I noticed a new stack of papers in front of him. The first couple of times I met with him, I felt overwhelmed and intimidated, but now I looked forward to our sessions and new things to learn.

I filled him in about my interactions with RJ and Cindy.

"That is absolutely brilliant," Dr. Richardson replied. "I really think you're getting this project management thing."

"Well, sometimes I still feel like I'm guessing," I admitted.

"That's totally normal, and I would definitely say follow your gut. You have great instincts."

"That's a relief," I said with a sigh. "I really believe my ideas for the music distribution will be a benefit, but I also need RJ to be on board. If I get a positive report from the orchestra committee, I believe it will go a long way."

"I couldn't agree with you more," replied Dr. Richardson. "Please keep me updated."

"I will," I said. "So, what do you have for me today?"

"Today I want to go over strategic management."

He briefly reviewed what we had discussed the previous week.

"If I'm going too fast, please let me know," he said.

"I'm following you," I replied. "I reviewed all those resource materials and articles you give me."

Dr. Richardson handed me the stack of papers.

"For each of the strategic process groups, I've also created a mind map (see Figure 5.1), along with the information about each of the processes. Today I'm going to cover developing a portfolio strategic plan, developing the portfolio charter, defining the portfolio roadmap, and managing strategic change."

My eyes got wide.

"I know it looks like a lot," he continued. "But just bear with me. You'll want to focus and almost memorize each process and their inputs, tools and techniques, and outputs. A part of understanding the portfolio management processes is to understand those sixteen processes, but in order to understand each of those processes, we've talked about the inputs, the outputs, and the tools and techniques that go into each one."

"My brain isn't as pliant as it was back in college," I said. "Do you have any recommendations on how to memorize it?"

"I can tell you how I did it," answered Dr. Richardson. "I used a memory technique where I had sixteen areas that I mapped out in my house and I assigned one of the portfolio processes to each area. And

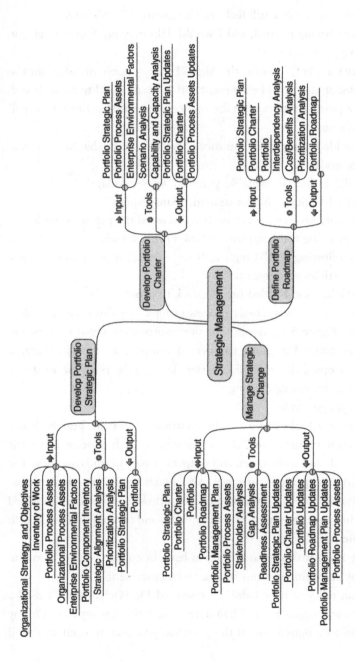

Figure 5.1 Strategic management mind map.

then as I walked through the house, into a room or into the garage, I would put up sticky notes in those areas to anchor the concepts of what I was learning. It helped me not only to memorize the sixteen processes in order, but also to memorize the various inputs, tools, and outputs for each of those sixteen processes."

"Oh, I like that," I said. "I'm writing that one down."

He pointed at the next page. (See Figure 5.2.)

"Developing links between vision, mission, objectives, strategies, and action plans, which are programs and projects, is critical to strategic alignment. The strategic alignment question to consider when evaluating the linkage process is: Does the project build value for the organization? Is the investment aligned with the organization's enterprise architecture and core technologies? Does the project create organizational effectiveness? Is the organization capable of implementing the process successfully? Think about how this applies to your project of music distribution."

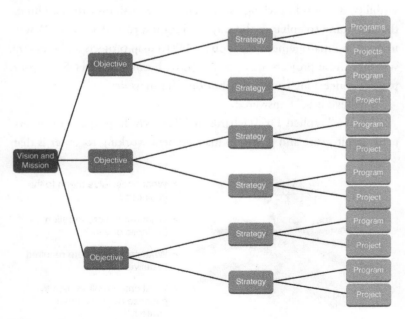

Figure 5.2 Strategic linkage.

I thought about it. It wasn't just the buy-in by the symphony. I needed to have a repeatable process for everyone to follow and it needed to be clear.

"Let's talk a little bit about business value," Dr. Richardson continued. "Business value is defined as the entire value of the business. What's the business worth? It is the total sum of all tangible and intangible assets. Here are some questions to consider when you're thinking about understanding the role that you're going to have to play as a portfolio manager and helping to manage business value."

He pointed to the next paper in the stack. (See Figure 5.3.)

"Each business that you're a part of will have a different definition based on its vision, mission, goals, objectives, where it's trying to go and what it's trying to do, and who it's trying to serve. And so you have to understand what value means to the symphony."

I'd have to think about that a bit.

"Business drivers are items like reduce costs, improve profits, increase visibility, develop knowledge share. Those are business drivers. Things that are going to enhance the way the business runs. And there's a way in portfolio management that you're able to map projects and measure whether those projects are affecting those business drivers. So is your project concerning music distribution a business driver?"

"I believe it is," I answered.

"I agree," replied Dr. Richardson. "The whole purpose of enterprise architecture and portfolio management working together is that

➢ What does value mean to the business?

➢ What are the organization's business drivers?

➢ What capabilities are required to deliver value?

➢ What criteria will we use to prioritize our investment strategy?

Figure 5.3   Understanding business value.

enterprise architecture looks at what types of things we have in place right now. Think of it this way: with enterprise architecture and portfolio management, when it comes to this capability concept, it's like if I want to go from Pensacola, Florida, to Tampa, Florida – that's a long way, right? And so it depends on the capability I have. If I only have a bicycle, then that is not really going to work. If I have a car, then yes. Now, it's going to take probably seven or eight hours to get there. But if I could fly on a plane, if I had the capability to access an aircraft, I could be there within an hour."

"I've been thinking of ways to scan the music and how to distribute them through a database program so I can send the correct parts to the correct people. I believe that RJ will have to help me with that."

"So you need to have that in place before you can fully switch over to electronic copies of the music."

"Yes," I agreed. "I really appreciate your help because I felt like my idea would be easy to do since most people have email."

"Exactly. That is why we're discussing strategy," replied Dr. Richardson. "When you really think about the concept of business value and developing the capabilities to deliver the value, you have to think about it from a mechanical standpoint of what vehicle, what systems, what processes, what tools do we have that can get us there? So think of the bicycle as a tool or a process. Is that process capable of getting me to my destination in a timely manner? If it's not, then I need to upgrade that process. Whether it's upgraded from a bicycle to a car, or if I have to get there within an hour on a regular basis, then I'm going to be upgrading from a car to buying a plane ticket."

"I get it," I agreed and made some quick notes for myself.

"Next, consider what criteria you will use to prioritize your investment strategy. And criteria are along the lines of the business values on drivers, but it's taking the drivers to a different level." (See Figure 5.4.)

"Consider how much your drivers are reducing costs. Consider your music distribution. How much is it actually going to save the symphony not to have to mail and replace parts?"

I made a note to get those numbers together.

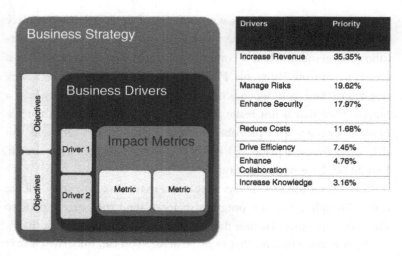

Figure 5.4 Selecting and prioritizing business drivers.

"Objectives must be specific in scope, action-oriented, and able to serve as high-level goals for an individual project," Dr. Richardson continued. "It should have been agreed upon through a consensus approach by as wide a group of senior managers and stakeholders as realistically possible. That's why going to your orchestra committee to survey the symphony is a great idea. You may want to talk to your board as well to get their take on it. You see, portfolio management takes a holistic view of an organization's strategy – both the business and executive leadership that project proposals by matching them with the company's strategic objectives."

I thought about some of my other ideas, such as arranging to get people paid by automatic deposit, and realized that similar surveying of the symphony might be a good idea.

"One of the key goals of this part of the portfolio management process is alignment among key leaders. Let's say you have the CIO, a CFO, a chief marketing officer, and a chief human resource officer. When you list out these business drivers – let's say increase revenue, manage risks, enhance security, reduce costs, drive efficiency, enhance collaboration, and increase knowledge – well, you can bet that the

CFO is going to be interested in increasing revenue and reducing costs. The CIO is going to be interested in enhancing security, possibly enhancing collaboration, increasing knowledge share. The human resource manager, well, they're going to be really interested in enhancing collaboration and increasing knowledge. What tends to happen is those leaders tend not to be on the same page as far as the priority of each of those drivers."

"You've worked with other companies. How do you get them on the same page?" I asked.

"I use a tool called the analytical hierarchy process," he said, as he shuffled through the stack and showed me a diagram. (See Figure 5.5.)

"It allows the various leaders to vote on the value and the priority of those drivers," he explained. "The algorithm on the backend basically calculates and then develops a unified view based on everyone's input

Pairwise Comparison Matrix

	=*Much* More Important	=*More* Important	The =*Same*	=*Less* Important	=*MuchLess* Important							
	9	3	1	0.333	0.111							

Criteria		Enhance Collaboration	Enhance Security	Increase Knowledge Share	Increase Revenue	Manage Risk	Reduce Cost					Total	%
	X	2	3	4	5	6	7	8	9	10	11	Total	%
Drive Efficiency	1											0.00	
Enhance Collaboration	2	X										0.00	
Enhance Security	3		X									0.00	
Increase Knowledge Share	4			X								0.00	
Increase Revenue	5				X							0.00	
Manage Risk	6					X						0.00	
Reduce Cost	7						X					0.00	
	8							X				0.00	
	9								X			0.00	
	10									X		0.00	
	11										X	0.00	
		0.00	0.00	0.00	0.00	0.00	0.00	0.00	0.00	0.00	0.00	0.00	0
												0	0.00

Figure 5.5   Analytic hierarchy process (AHP).

and then prioritizes the business drivers. It allows you to prioritize those drivers. And then the leaders can talk about it. One of the great benefits of portfolio management to the business is that it gets the leadership team on the same page when it comes to prioritization of the business activity, the business drivers, and the direction of the organization. Now I understand that this may not work with your symphony, but it's worth looking at and understanding. You're already doing these things on a smaller scale directly with the board and other departments."

So I was doing some things right. That was great to hear. Because of Laura's opposition to my job and my ability to do it, there were times I really doubted myself.

"Once you've gone through and prioritized your business drivers using the tools of the analytical hierarchy process, you want to identify the existing or new items that you want to put into your portfolio," Dr. Richardson continued. "I refer to these as components. A component can be a project. A component could be a portfolio or a sub-portfolio. A component could be a program. Or it could even be operational work that makes up the portfolio that you're putting together. Your music distribution plan is a component."

"I get it," I replied.

"You want to evaluate the current portfolio. You want to weed out the portfolio of projects not aligned with the corporate strategy. You also want to identify new proposed projects in the portfolio. You've already begun doing this, but you'll continue this weeding over time. And then, once you have those projects, you'll want to optimize and recalibrate to achieve an optimal value. Additionally, you want to ask these questions: How many projects can the organization absorb at one time? Does the organization have the capacity to deliver the selected portfolio? And does the portfolio need to be synchronized to adjust demand and provide buffering? You ran into this issue when you first made your proposal to the board."

"Even though that was only a few weeks ago, it feels like a lifetime ago," I said. "I've learned so much about portfolio management; I wish I could have a redo."

"I'm sure they knew you had to learn more about your position, and they seemed patient with you. Can you imagine how prepared you'll be with next year's budget?"

He was right. I had to cut myself a little slack. I needed to keep learning and improving. I just hoped Fernando, Sam, and the board could see the improvements.

"Now you have prioritized your business drivers, and you created a consensus among your leadership team," continued Dr. Richardson. "You've identified projects, existing projects, the new projects, and operational work that aligns to the organizational strategy because you've had these new business drivers that have been prioritized. The next thing you want to do is to categorize your project investment. How do you do that? I like to leverage the Gartner Framework for transforming, growing, and running the business."

I was taking furious notes. It seemed like a lot of pieces and parts for the symphony, but I wanted to learn portfolio management on a bigger scale in case I wanted to move into another position with a larger organization in the future.

"According to the Gartner Framework, when you transform the business, any projects that fit within the transform-the-business bucket, they are investments in new markets, ventures, mergers and acquisitions, new products, or outsourcing efforts." Dr. Richardson explained. "A transform business project is a project that is going to create disruption in the market or disruption in the company. A grow-the-business project is one you invest in to expand the company's scope of products and services, upgrade software, add incremental capabilities, and develop new skills. And then, the run-the-business projects are investments to keep the business operational, like maintenance contracts and disaster recovery contracts. So now we have a project portfolio of a collection of components that we've actually put into categories for investments and for investing in."

"Tell me more about the software and systems that you use to prioritize these projects," I encouraged him. (See Figure 5.6.)

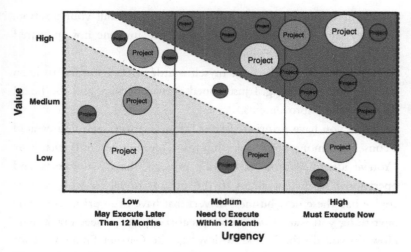

Figure 5.6   Project prioritization.

"There are tools like Microsoft Project Server, Portfolio Management Tool, and TransparentChoice. And there are other third-party
tools that you can use as well. But the idea is that once each project
has been evaluated against the objectives, the business drivers, KPIs,
and business benefit statements, it can be assigned to a strategic value.
And the system does that. And so, based on the system that you're
using, the bubbles placement and the size and color will depend on the
criteria you use when you're prioritizing your projects. And obviously,
in this scenario, everything that's in the upper right-hand corner in the
darker area has greater value to the business than the ones in the lower,
lighter-shaded area."

He then placed some other graphs in front of me. (See Figure 5.7.)

"This portfolio analysis tool is the Microsoft Project Server portfolio analysis tool that's inside of Project Server. It can help you to identify the strategic alignment of projects and to prioritize the projects.
You can create scenarios, probabilities, and cost-benefit analyses of
the entire portfolio, not just a single project. You can look at resource
capacity, and interdependencies between projects."

> Efficiency Frontier
> Strategic Alignment
> Prioritization
> Scenario
> Probability

> Cost/Benefit
> Resource Capacity
> Interdependency
> Business Value

Figure 5.7 Portfolio analysis.

It looked intimidating, but I was developing goals. Perhaps some of this software could be used as I developed more projects.

"With the portfolio analysis, you're rationalizing the portfolio. It's necessary to ensure that it does not contain multiple projects that are superfluous or mutually exclusive. Each category of benefits should be consolidated to evaluate whether the target KPIs can be achieved. Portfolio optimization considers the organization's constraints, money, resources, time, and level of risk. The cost-benefit analysis seeks to define the benefit that will be provided by the portfolio and compares it to the cost of the portfolio programs and projects."

"This cost-benefit analysis sheet is per project. It is not only important to look at just the investments and the cost-benefit analysis of the single project. It is important to consider the cost-benefit analysis of the entire portfolio as well."

"The portfolio roadmap is the investment roadmap, which provides a short-, medium-, and long-term view of the portfolio investment strategy. The roadmap facilitates dialogue and builds an agreement on the organization's funding and resource allocation plan, as well as its alignment to goals and objectives."

This would be extremely important as I built and worked on next year's budget.

"Are you getting all this?" Dr. Richardson asked.

"Most of it," I admitted.

"There is a lot to absorb, I know. Here are some more *Harvard Business Review* articles that might help you." I took a stack of articles neatly stapled and put them in a separate pile.

"Here is a checklist that I think will help you understand the process a bit better," he said. (See Figure 5.8.)

"This is a process that can be used for each project," he said. "To be managed as a project, you need to start off with a charter for the portfolio management practice. You need to have an executive sponsor, whether it's the CIO or a partner, or someone at the C level who can help shepherd this through because it will require a major culture change in your organization. In your case, it would be the board and your director, Sam. You also have to develop a project plan or implementation plan and then clarify roles and responsibilities. You are doing that with RJ and Cindy. I would recommend using a RACI chart."

"What is that?" I asked.

As a project:
1. Charter the PPM project and secure executive sponsorship.
2. Develop a project plan.
3. Clarify roles and responsibilities.
4. Evaluate the current portfolio and conduct gap analysis.
5. Weed out projects not aligned to the strategy.
6. Develop the PPM processes.
7. Select and implement the PPM tools.
8. Conduct training.
9. Conduct a pilot.
10. Mentor, coach, and conduct an audit.
11. Expand the pilot and roll out to remaining users.

Figure 5.8 Steps to implement a PPM practice.

"It's a chart that covers the areas of responsible, accountable, consulted, and informed around the processes of things that you have to deal with."

"Makes sense," I said.

"Then you have to evaluate the current portfolio and conduct a portfolio gap analysis to see where you are. One of the things that I use is a maturity model assessment to do this. It really helps to identify what the gaps are in an organization and then helps them to get aligned to that."

"Next, you will want to weed out products that are not aligned to the strategy, which we just talked about. This is followed by developing your portfolio management processes and selecting and implementing a tool. You can use a spreadsheet for the symphony. I believe you have already started one."

"I have," I replied.

"If you were working for a much larger organization, I would recommend using an enterprise system that's been created and built for that. Then you would roll out some sort of training that speaks to the executive team to coach them through the process and help them understand their role as executives and executive sponsors of projects and portfolios, followed by coaching the portfolio managers, the PMO, and being very clear about which PMO you're talking about. In the case of your music distribution, it will be clear that you need to teach RJ."

I hoped that RJ was going to be on board and not resistant to the new process should it get that far.

"Then you want to conduct a pilot of your portfolio process. In this case, you'll pick a concert and try out the new process. You'll continue mailing music and try the new approach with a sample of the orchestra. You don't want to quit the old system and implement the new one all at once without testing it. I recommend trying the pilot for a few concerts to work out the bugs before replacing the old system entirely. By running a pilot, you create a center of excellence of people who understand the new process, all the terminology, the ways you're going to leverage the systems, and the tools you're going to introduce.

"You will also need some coaching and mentoring and you'll have to conduct an audit of your environment over time. Because once you build out the portfolio, you're constantly having to go back through it and report on what you're doing. You constantly have to recalibrate the portfolio, especially if there's a market shift, if there are new directions or new changes to the strategy because of a storm or any kind of act of God or things that happen. Or there could be a major disruption in the business or in the market that you have to reply to very quickly. You need to be able to do that."

"I understand," I said. "I really appreciate this."

"Do you have any questions?" Dr. Richardson asked.

"As I've been reading the articles and hearing you today, I wonder: Does the project portfolio management process work as a bridge, or is it a hub?" (See Figure 5.9.)

"Great question," he replied. "It's one I get often."

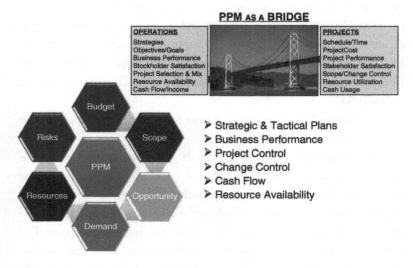

Figure 5.9 Is PPM a bridge or a hub?
Credit: Luciano Mortula-LGM/Adobe Stock

"A bridge basically connects operations and strategy to projects," explained Dr. Richardson. "But the hub-and-spoke concept is that you have portfolio management in the middle, and it touches all of these areas, like risk and budget and scope, resources, and demand. Harvey Levine, who wrote an important book on project portfolio management, takes the position that portfolio management is not a bridge, but it's a hub that acts as a decision support environment that provides access to all the information across an organization, the ability to provide analytical insights, a vehicle for communication, alignment of investments to organizational objectives, and a platform for controlling risk."

"I see," I replied.

"Whenever you're thinking about the role that you're going to play when you take the position of portfolio manager in an organization, you become the center part of a wheel where you're touching budget, risk, scope, and alignment of products and programs. You really help to move things along. Again, if you use that analogy of the corpus callosum I mentioned to you last week, you're taking the vision of the organization and helping the part of the body that can execute it or create actions around it to get those things done. That becomes a really critical part of any business to have a well-oiled portfolio management process and for you to be a top-notch, elite portfolio management practitioner."

"Well, that's my goal," I said. "To be a top-notch practitioner."

"I have to say, within record time you have grasped concepts that most of my grad students struggle with."

"I really appreciate that. I have my work cut out for me," I said. "Same time next week?"

"You bet."

As I got into my car, I thought about everything that had been going on this week. I came to the conclusion that I really needed to get my personal life sorted out to have any chance of keeping my new position under control. Projects were going to begin to overlap, and I needed to be on my A-game. I couldn't do that if my marriage and family were falling apart.

Dr. Richardson's Tips

- Developing links between vision, mission, objectives, strategies, and action plans, which are programs and projects, is critical to strategic alignment. The strategic alignment question to consider when evaluating the linkage process is: Does the project build value for the organization? Is the investment aligned with the organization's enterprise architecture and core technologies? Does the project create organizational effectiveness? Is the organization capable of implementing the process successfully?

- Objectives must be specific in scope, action-oriented, and able to serve as high-level goals for an individual project. It should have been agreed upon through a consensus approach by as wide a group of senior managers and stakeholders as realistically possible.

- You can evaluate the current portfolio and conduct a portfolio gap analysis to see where you are. One of the things that I use is a maturity model assessment to do this. It really helps to identify what the gaps are in an organization and then helps them to get aligned to that.

CHAPTER 6

CHOOSING YOUR RULES OF ENGAGEMENT

Jerry wants to get the symphony to adopt direct deposit for payment. The current system requires two signatures on a check that is often not ready until the Monday after the concert. The players are not happy with this arrangement, and sometimes they receive checks a week or more after the concert. To implement this new program, Jerry must get approval from the board and get people's banking information (some don't have bank accounts and must set one up). There is buy-in from the players, but the conductor does not want to give up rehearsal time to allow Jerry to explain the changes and get people to fill out bank forms. The implementation is a little bumpy during the first concert, and there are a few checks that need to be written. Also, Jerry had not factored in sub-players who might not have had time to fill out their bank info and get into the system.

Jerry slips and injures his arm. He can't play, but he can continue to work in his new position.

Linda apologizes for her recent slips in behavior. She is home more. Corey and Linda help Jerry at home. Laura becomes more involved in volunteer work and is not at home as much as she used to be.

"I don't see any fractures," said the ER doctor. "But I believe you have torn your rotator cuff."

This was the worst news. The absolute worse. A broken collarbone would have been better. At least that would heal, and I could go on playing. A torn rotator cuff could be a career-ender.

"How bad is it?" I asked.

"It's hard to tell with the swelling," the doctor replied. "We won't know for a few weeks. I'm going to refer you to an orthopedic doctor, who will be able to give you a better idea."

"Will I need surgery?" I asked. My stomach was in my throat. I wished I didn't have to deal with this on my own, but Laura wasn't available because she was on the other side of town volunteering at the moment.

"Not right now. Again, we will know better when the swelling is down. We'll need to immobilize it, and you'll need to ice it for the next few days. You can take an over-the-counter anti-inflammatory, or I can write you a prescription."

My shoulder hurt. A lot. But I didn't want to have to take a heavy-duty painkiller. I needed my brain to be clear.

"No, I'll be fine," I said.

"The nurse will be in with your sling and discharge papers."

"Thank you very much," I said as he left.

I picked up my phone with my good hand.

"Call Laura," I said to the AI.

There was loud music playing in the background when she answered.

"Where are you?" I asked.

"I told you I was volunteering today. And we are also having a surprise birthday luncheon for Sarah at Marty's Grill."

I tried to disguise my anxiety and worries I was sitting in the emergency room with a serious injury, and Laura wasn't here with me.

"No, I don't remember you telling me that. I just saw the doctor," I said loudly.

"I can't hear you," Laura said. "Can you just text me?"

Before I could answer, she hung up, so we exchanged a series of texts.

ME: *I just finished seeing the doctor.*

LAURA: *And?*

ME: *And I tore my rotator cuff. It's bad. I won't be able to play for weeks, perhaps months, and it could require surgery.*

There was a long pause.

ME: *Are you there?*

LAURA: *Yeah, sorry that that this has happened to you. There's a lot going on here.*

ME: *There is a lot going on here too. I might not be able to play for a long time. Perhaps ever.*

LAURA: *I'm not sure what you want me to do.*

ME: *Well, as my wife, I need you here. They are immobilizing my arm and I won't be able to drive.*

LAURA: *I am all the way across town. Can't you call a cab?*

ME: *I can't believe this. Not only will I not be able to drive today, but I also won't be able to drive for weeks.*

LAURA: *Even if I leave right now, with the traffic it's going to take me an hour to get there. You're better off taking a cab. It's not like you're dying. I will also have to rearrange my schedule and cancel a bunch of stuff. The timing of this isn't good.*

I was thankful I wasn't talking on the phone because I might have said things I'd regret later.

ME: *It is not as if I planned it.*

LAURA: *Well, at least you have that other job thingy you are doing.*

ME: *I don't know what is going to happen. If I have surgery, I won't be able to do much of anything for a while.*

Again, there was a long pause with three dots blinking.

LAURA: *Listen, I got to go now if I need to pick up the kids. I don't want to be rude with my friends here. I will talk to you about this later when I get home.*

I was livid and hurt that I had to face this alone and she wasn't here with me.

I took a few breaths to compose myself before the nurse reentered. I guess Laura was right; I was going to have to figure a few things out. This was bad, and I felt a wave of despair threatening to overtake me.

★ ★ ★

"Sam, thanks for meeting with me on short notice," I said, sitting down in his office. It had been three days since my injury, and I was rethinking my moment of bravery in not getting a prescription for pain. It was keeping me up at night. I had to move to the spare bedroom because Laura was complaining I was keeping her up. The twin bed was a torture rack from medieval times.

"What happened?" he asked with a shocked expression.

"It's been many years since I've been skateboarding, and I am longer good at it," I laughed.

"You went skateboarding?"

"Not willingly. Corey had left his board near the door of the garage. I was in a hurry and had not turned on the light on the way to my car. I stepped on the skateboard, and my arm went the wrong way when I fell. I've torn my rotator cuff."

"Ouch, that sounds terrible," Sam replied.

"It wasn't fun," I said. "That's why I wanted to talk to you. I don't know how long I'm going to be out of play. I've already called Claudia, and she will be the principal for the upcoming season. She is fully capable. If I can play later in the season, I'll just sub in one of the other chairs."

"What can we do for you?" asked Sam with a concerned face.

"I wanted to assure you – personally – that I will still be able to ful-fill my duties as the personnel manager. In some strange way, not play-ing is actually a little blessing, so I can concentrate more on that job."

"You know, if you need time, you can take it," replied Sam.

While this was a tempting offer, I was afraid they would simply replace me. I had been working so hard I didn't want to give up now.

"I believe, for now, I will be fine," I replied. "If something changes, I'll let you know right away."

"Okay, but know that your health and well-being come first. Are you sure there's nothing we can do for you?"

"There is one thing," I said. I was almost embarrassed to ask. "Can you break the news to Fernando? He doesn't take bad news well, and I just don't have the bandwidth right now to deal with him."

Sam grinned. "No problem. I know how to deal with him."

"I really appreciate it." I stood up. "I'd shake your hand, but . . ."

"Get on out of here," Sam chuckled.

★ ★ ★

It had been a week since my fall, and I just ached. I didn't want to complain, so I kept my discomfort to myself. I was afraid I was taking enough Ibuprofen to burn a hole in my stomach.

"It's going to be okay, Dad," said Linda.

She had been a champ this week. She helped with cooking, and helped me get around. She even drove me places after school. She had only recently gotten her license and was a good driver, but I kept my eyes closed most of the time.

"I hate that you took off school to take me to this appointment," I said.

"I know you're nervous about the surgery, so I wanted to be there for you," she said. "I told my teachers I'd be out today, so I already have my work."

This seemed unfair to me because it should have been Laura taking me to the appointment. She made an excuse to help her parents move stuff around, and she had already promised them twice and couldn't say no a third time. It wasn't worth the fight, but it was something I would bring up in therapy.

"I really do appreciate it," I said. "I talked to your counselor yesterday, and she said you've made a miracle turnaround on your grades. You have no idea how happy that makes me."

"You were right, Dad," she said, as we pulled into the parking lot.

"Wait . . . wait . . . can you say that again in the mic?" I said jokingly.

"Seriously, Dad. I know I've been a real pain. And my friends weren't helping any. I see how hard you're working for us, and I know it's been affecting your time at home, so I figured it was time for me to be more responsible."

"That, and your grades are attached to your driving privileges and going out on the weekends," I reminded her.

"Yeah, but that isn't my motivation. I'm mad at Mom for how she's been treating you lately, and now with your hurt shoulder, you need help."

"It isn't your responsibility," I replied.

"Maybe it's not, but I want to help."

I gave her a hug across the seat.

"Are we ready to do this thing?" she asked.

"No, but let's do it anyway."

★ ★ ★

"So, Sam tells me you aren't playing this season?" said Fernando with a slight scowl as he stared at me across his desk.

"I had an accident," I replied. "I saw the orthopedist yesterday, and we talked about options. We're going to let it heal and try some physical therapy to get it back into shape. I might still need surgery later, but this seems the best way forward. What that means is that I won't be able to play next season. Claudia will do fine in my position. I'll bring in one of the alternates to fill the hole in the section."

"That sounds fine," he replied.

"I wanted to talk to you about the new system for paying the musicians," I said.

"I'm going to stop you right there," Fernando replied. "I am not involved in any of the money stuff. You will need to talk to Sam and the board about all that."

"Yes, I understand that," I replied. "But I could use your support. I need to talk to the musicians at the first rehearsal about making sure they get me their tax forms and the direct deposit information so that they can be paid."

"So, are you saying they won't get paid if they don't?"

"No, we're going to do this gradually, the first few concerts. I'd like most if not all the musicians on direct deposit by the end of the season."

"Okay," he replied. "Is there anything else I can help you with?"

This was my dismissal, and so I took the cue.

"No," I said. "I just wanted to touch base with you."

"In the future, I'd prefer you come to me with personnel changes rather than going through Sam. I am fine with your decision, but you need to let me know right away."

"Yes, of course," I said and moved as quickly as I could out of his office. He was a great conductor but just not a people person, at least not to his musicians and staff. The donors loved him, and he really knew how to turn on the charm when he wanted to. I wished he could use that charm when talking to me.

* * *

"I'm sorry I had to reschedule," I said to Dr. Richardson. "This has been a rough couple of weeks."

"Not a problem at all," he replied. "Is your arm healing?"

"Yes, but I'm afraid it's going to be a slow process," I said. "I am taking it day by day."

"I hated to hear you won't be playing this upcoming season."

"Like I said to Sam, this might be a small blessing. I can work on my project management skills."

"I'm glad to hear it," Dr. Richardson replied.

"I got the approval from the board to move forward with the direct deposit. I'm taking it slow."

"What has the response been?"

"There are two distinct camps. There are those who feel that we should have done this years ago, and they're thrilled that their funds will be available to them on the day of the concert. And then there are those who feel like it will mess up or that they don't trust technology. Included are those musicians who don't even have a bank account. I was amazed at this."

"How have they been getting along without it?" Dr. Richardson asked.

"They would just cash the checks they received. Now they'll have to open up a bank account for the first time. There were so many that I asked First Bank of Middle Village to come in to help set up accounts for the musicians. We've arranged a day the musicians can come in to meet with people from the bank, and they're giving them good rates because they're sponsors of the symphony."

"That is a brilliant idea."

"I have to say, learning more about project management has changed my way of thinking. I'm looking at all sides of projects and coming up with solutions as challenges arrive. In this case, it's reducing the musicians' anxiety and, at the same time, removing the barrier of them having an excuse not to use direct deposit. Many other symphonies and musical organizations, including the choral society here, are moving to direct deposit, so it's really helping the musicians beyond our organization."

"You are so right, and it adds to the value for the musicians to be a part of the organization," said Dr. Richardson. "I'd give you a high-five, but . . ."

We both laughed.

He brought out a new stack of papers for me to study. At first I was overwhelmed by the idea of homework and learning so much, but then I began to look forward to it. I was applying what I was learning, and the results were amazing.

"Today I'm going to talk to you about governance, which is the process of putting policies, procedures, and processes in place to guide organizational, operational activities and change. Governance should provide a streamlined approach and process. If governance becomes a bottleneck, then there's something wrong with the design of the governance processes. So the goal of governance is to make things run faster, not to become a bottleneck."

He slid over the stack of papers. (See Figure 6.1.) "I want us to review the five processes that make up the portfolio governance

Knowledge Area	Defining Process Group	Aligning Process Group	Authoring and Controlling Process Group
Portfolio Strategic Management	4.1 Develop Portfolio Strategic Plan 4.2 Develop Portfolio Charter 4.3 Define Portfolio Roadmap	4.4 Manage Strategic Change	
Portfolio Governance	5.1 Develop Portfolio Management Plan 5.2 Define Portfolio	5.3 Optimize Portfolio	5.4 Authorize Portfolio 5.5 Provide Portfolio Oversight
Portfolio Performance Management	6.1 Develop Portfolio Performance Management Plan	6.2 Manage Supply and Demand 6.3 Manage Portfolio Value	
Portfolio Communication Management	7.1 Develop Portfolio Communication Management Plan	7.2 Manage Portfolio Information	
Portfolio Risk Management	8.1 Develop Portfolio Risk Management Plan	8.2 Manage Portfolio Risk	

Figure 6.1 Portfolio management process group.

process group, and those processes are to develop a portfolio management plan, define the portfolio, optimize the portfolio, authorize the portfolio, and provide portfolio oversight. I believe this lesson is timely because you ran into a couple of issues concerning governance when you were setting up the direct deposit."

"Like the last time we met, I've created a mind map that outlines the five processes. It also provides the detailed inputs, tools, and techniques needed for operationalizing each of these processes." (See Figure 6.2.)

The more he went over the different aspects of portfolio management, the more it made sense. I only wish I had met with him before I had started my position, but I was glad to have the guidance now.

"As I stated earlier, governance is the process of putting policies, procedures, and processes in place to guide organizational and operational activities and changes. Governance warrants the achievement of an organization's objectives by strategically aligning daily activities, setting direction, providing guidance on decision-making, and monitoring performance."

"That's a lot to digest," I said.

"Let me tell you a quick story," Dr. Richardson said. "Before I was a professor, I was a planning and programs manager for an international law firm. In addition to being in charge of the project program and portfolio management groups, I also oversaw the governance processes. We had at least six or seven boards and committees. The boards were able to make decisions, and committees could provide input but could not make decisions – much like your orchestra committee, which takes the issues of the musicians to your board."

I nodded in understanding.

"We laid out a process where we orchestrated all of the boards where it was very clear that one board fed information to the project review board, the project review board would feed information to the monthly IS committee, and then both of those committees fed information to the IT strategy committee – and so on. On the board that the CIO chaired, there were operational committees, and in addition, there was a change board and a service board. And because we

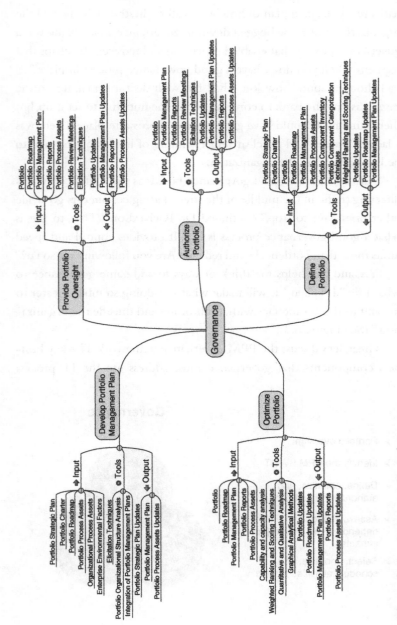

Figure 6.2 Governance mind map.

had a really detailed plan of how it was all orchestrated, it allowed the organization not to be bogged down in governance, but it really was a governance process that enabled execution and reduced the chaos that happens when you don't have a good governance process in place."

I thought about how lost I had felt with decision-making. In the case of asking the bank to come in, I took the initiative to set it up, but then Sam said I should have gotten board approval in place. There was a lack of process and no clear understanding of how projects were to be handled within the organization.

"I always think of good governance boards as the traffic cop who's directing traffic in the middle of the street, letting certain cars go while other ones have to stop," continued Dr. Richardson. "That, to me, is what a good governance process is like. It provides control and speed limits more than bottlenecks and red tape. Are you following me so far?"

"Yes, and this helps me think of ways to add some governance to what I do," I replied. "It will make what I'm doing so much clearer to me and to those I interact with, both inside and outside the organization." (See Figure 6.3.)

"Great, let's discuss the PPM governance framework. The key business components that governance must address are the IT process

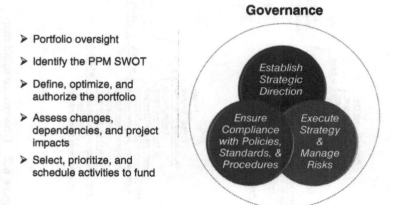

Figure 6.3   Establish a PPM governance framework.

optimization, alignment between IT goals and business goals, enterprise architecture capability engagement, demand management, IT performance management and tracking, portfolio program, project oversight, and board committee development and monitoring. And so, the governance boards establish direction, oversee strategy execution or the execution of the strategy of managing risks, and ensure compliance with the policies, procedures, and standards. You have to have a solid framework for implementing your governance process." (See Figure 6.4.)

"Makes sense," I replied.

"The governance framework provides the structure to enable decisions to be made regarding IT and business investments. Governance provides the process that defines what decisions are made, who makes them, how results are measured when they are made, who's held accountable for those decisions, and how decisions are made and monitored. Every organization has an IT governance structure. The question is, is the governance process defined, or is it ad hoc?"

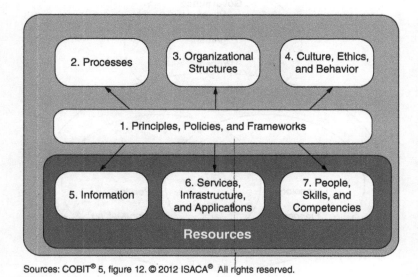

Figure 6.4   Governance framework.

"In the symphony, I believe it is more ad hoc."

"Precisely. Productive and profitable organizations have a well-defined and well-managed governance process. The policies, processes, and procedures are key when you're rolling out a project portfolio measure office or governance structure. And these things should include determining roles and responsibilities, identifying and documenting the process for governance and the IT portfolio management process."

Again, I thought about my rolling out the new direct deposit plan. Dr. Richardson was right; if there was a more defined governance process, I would not be floundering around so much or be so worried about violating some protocol, even though there didn't seem to be any well-defined protocols. I felt I was walking on eggshells at times.

Dr. Richardson pointed to the next page in the stack. (See Figure 6.5.)

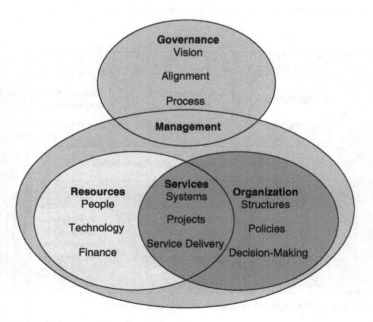

Figure 6.5   Portfolio governance model.

"Remember, the project portfolio process or office is a hub and not a bridge. Determine and define the governance compliance triggers so that you know when a process or a procedure has been violated and determine and establish the organizational model required to support and sustain the project portfolio capability."

It was like he was reading my mind.

"One example of a good policy or process or procedure is when I worked with the international law firm," he continued. "I had developed a handbook that included a list of all the steps and processes, and procedures for managing small, medium, and large projects. It also explained how the business and the IT management and leadership team were to interact with the project review board, and when to submit project requests."

"Yes . . . yes," I blurted. "I need one of those."

Dr. Richardson chuckled. "I can help you with that."

"That would be fantastic," I replied.

"My project managers did not fear stepping away to go to the bathroom. They didn't fear not being able to go to lunch because they knew no one could come up to them and just assign them a project; they had to follow a process. So, as work was divvied out, they were able to remain focused on their work, and the business knew that if they submitted their requests to my office, they would get a response because all those projects were presented to the project review board on a weekly basis."

"This portfolio governance model provides an example of only one kind of model that can be used in an organization where you have a separate governance process, the management role, and then resources, services, and the overall organizational structure. The IT group itself can be divided into this, and as you can see, senior leadership will play a part in identifying and defining the portfolio governance model because the areas that we're looking at and that are a part of this model are things that fall under the manager's and managing director's purview."

I looked at the chart as he continued.

"The good news is that, as the personnel manager and in essence a portfolio manager, you get a seat at the table and get a chance to work with them day in and day out as you help them support and manage the portfolio."

"Here's another example of a portfolio governance operational model. (See Figure 6.6.) We have resources; we have the overall environment or technical environment; we have the governance and administration where we have the boards and committees and contracts and budgets and metrics. And then we have a portfolio center of excellence where it's responsible for education and training. So there are multiple types of governance processes that are out there, and you have to define one that fits the culture that you're working in and that fits the future direction of where your organization wants to go as far as managing its project portfolio process and overseeing all of its portfolio assets."

"This might take some time," I commented.

"Yes, of course. But it is a goal you can begin to work on with the symphony to develop over time," replied Dr. Richardson. "I've added a couple of other templates in your packet that you can look over later. One is called the portfolio management plan, and the other one is called the portfolio review meeting agenda. The review meeting

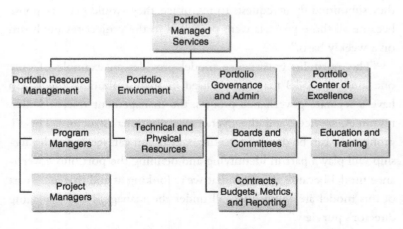

Figure 6.6 Portfolio governance operational model.

agenda is used when managing the portfolio review board. And the portfolio management plan is a document that you build out when you're first establishing your portfolio management office. Basically, it's a plan that you use to govern and manage how you're going to manage the portfolio overall."

"Those will be helpful," I said.

"As a project manager," Dr. Richardson continued, "you're responsible for on-time delivery of a project, keeping within the scope and on budget. You're also responsible for managing multiple projects and then delivering the benefits that all of those products being worked on together should be able to deliver as well as managing your limited resources. But when you become a portfolio manager, one of the main roles or jobs that you have is to constantly look at the portfolio and see if you can optimize the portfolio. And optimizing the portfolio is one of the key activities for the PML and to add value to the business. It's the core concern that optimization is the delivery of a strategic value while reducing the cost of delivering that value through streamlining the use of resources. That's money, people, information, and equipment while increasing the speed at which the benefits are produced. Right now, you are doing a bit of both roles. But, as you begin to create a framework, you will have a much easier time managing your resources."

I was overwhelmed with all of the duties I had on my shoulders at the moment, but every project was a little easier as I began to understand how project management works. (See Figure 6.7.)

"If there are projects that you have within your portfolio that you know if you really focused on those that they would deliver benefit to the organization much faster, then you as the portfolio manager should have the authority to fast-track or have those products focused on because your focus and your job are to optimize the portfolio to deliver the highest level of value while reducing the cost and risk to the organization. Now, the project portfolio management governs decision process; it's basically looking at the life cycle of your portfolio. There are different types of meetings and different types of decisions

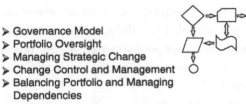

> Governance Model
> Portfolio Oversight
> Managing Strategic Change
> Change Control and Management
> Balancing Portfolio and Managing
>   Dependencies
> Performance, Risk, and Communication
>   Planning
> Procurement Planning
> Portfolio Prioritization Modeling

Figure 6.7   Elements of the portfolio management plan.

that you should be having as part of managing the portfolio. So you should have strategic planning meetings, you should have portfolio office meetings, and then you have the projects and programs that you are overseeing that are a part of your portfolio. I know this sounds like a lot right now, but as you grow into your role, you will be prepared."

"Yes, thanks to your guidance," I replied.

He showed me the next page. (See Figure 6.8.)

"As you can see, some meetings for portfolio strategic planning focus on the C-level group, which usually happens annually, like your initial budget meeting. Nowadays, because of the speed of business, it may happen every six months or even every quarter. The portfolio

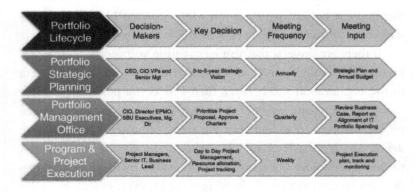

Figure 6.8   PPM governance decision process.

office meetings where you are recalibrating the portfolio and approving projects into the portfolio and aligning it and so on, those happen quarterly. And again, depending on the business that you're in, that could even happen monthly. And programs are basically day-to-day operational work, and it's how the project portfolio gets executed. It's through the projects and programs, and those are weekly meetings that are being executed and discussed. And this lays out who are the stakeholders, the decision-makers and what key decisions are made, how frequently they're made and what are the meeting inputs."

"This is helpful," I said.

"Let's move on to project portfolio management governance project review board process. Take your time studying this process. This shows you how projects build through the project review board and the portfolio review board to be approved within an organization."

He pointed at the page. (See Figure 6.9.)

"Here are the objectives of the project intake process. Let's talk about how you set up a streamlined standard process for intaking in new projects and looking at them against the portfolio. You have to identify project ideas that can contribute to the commencement of the strategic objectives; you reduce the number of projects so that you have an optimal size based on the company's capability to deliver."

"That is tough right now because some of these projects need to happen while others can wait," I said. "But it still feels like I need to complete a lot of projects in a short amount of time."

"You'll get the hang of it, and next year you'll be more prepared. The thing that kills most organizations is when they take on too many projects and struggle to deliver on them. The business and the people they are rolling these projects out to can't absorb all the change. I think you have a good pace right now, even though it feels like a lot. Sometimes to speed up, we have to slow down. We also need to eliminate products that are not feasible anymore. Sometimes you start a project, and you invest money into it, and then technology changes. This was the process that allowed my project managers at the international offer to feel very comfortable going out to lunch, going to

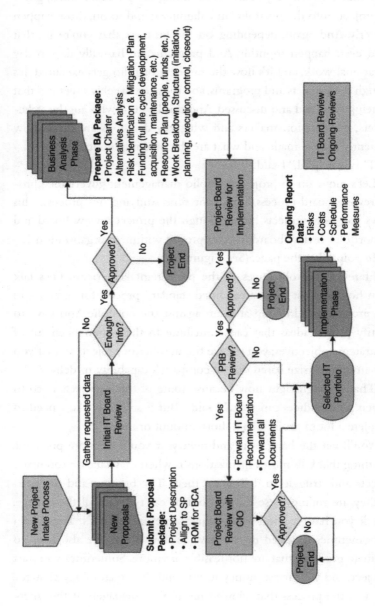

Figure 6.9 PPM governance project review board process.

the bathroom, and doing whatever they had to do because they didn't have to worry about someone chasing them down in the hallway so that they would have to get a new project and hide away. It freed them up to do their job."

"That will be a nice feeling," I said.

"Imagine kids going onto a school bus – their parents line them up one by one to enter the bus so they don't all run to the door at the same time. And because they have these heavy backpacks on, they get caught, and they're not able to get on the bus as quickly, and parents have to come and pull them back and put them back in line. Even though the straight line seems like a slow process, it actually lets them get on the bus much faster because of the way it's organized. And the whole concept of the theory of constraints, especially around portfolio management, is to reduce bottlenecks. Because bottlenecks reveal issues within the system that prohibit throughput and inventory and operating in an optimal manner."

I thought about some of the bottlenecks I was running into just this week.

"The theory of constraints is a solution for planning, scheduling, and managing the performance of a project environment," explained Dr. Richardson. "It is applied in both single projects and multi-project environments, where resources are shared across several different projects concurrently. The longest string of work is a schedule taking into account all tasks, resources, and dependencies. The goal is to reduce the demand to within a reasonable limit of the organization's capacity to meet the demand."

I was thinking about all he said and looked at the copious notes I had taken.

"That should do you," said Dr. Richardson.

"Yeah, I'd say so," I replied.

"Please take care of yourself," Dr. Richardson said with a concerned look. "Without your health and well-being, what do you have?"

He had a good point. While I was concerned about my shoulder and my future as a bass player, I was more concerned about my wife and family. I needed to make time to work on it, and I hoped that Laura hadn't pulled too far away from me.

Dr. Richardson's Tips

- As a project manager, you're responsible for the on-time delivery of a project, keeping within the scope and on budget. You're also responsible for managing multiple projects, and then delivering the benefits that all of those products being worked on together should be able to deliver, as well as managing your limited resources.

- Here are the objectives of the project intake process. You have to identify project ideas that can contribute to the commencement of the strategic objectives; you reduce the number of projects so that you have an optimal size based on the company's capability to deliver.

- The theory of constraints is a solution for planning, scheduling, and managing the performance of a project environment. It is applied in both single projects and multi-project environments, where resources are shared across several different projects concurrently.

CHAPTER 7

CHOOSING YOUR PERFORMANCE METRICS

"It's important that the musicians are on time next week for the fundraiser," said Sam.

"Yeah, about that, I'm having some trouble finding people to come," I replied.

"What? It's only a week away."

My stomach sank. I had been dreading this conversation.

"You did tell them they could eat afterward?" added Sam.

"Yes, but . . ."

"They do understand how important this event is, right? If the musicians want a raise, then we need the donors to give."

I had practiced in my head what I was going to say. I didn't want to have another tirade as I had with the board a few months ago. I took a couple of breaths.

"Are the waitstaff going to be paid? Bartenders? Are you paying for the food and drink?"

"We have donors and sponsors covering those things," Sam replied with a little irritation.

"But the waitstaff, cooks, and other people are not working for free," I replied.

"No, but that's different. They don't work for the symphony. That's how they make a living," said Sam.

I just looked at him without saying anything. I let his last words hang in the air rather than immediately responding, hoping he would consider what he was saying.

He sighed. He got it.

"It doesn't make sense for me to tell the players they are working for a raise while at the same time asking them to play for free."

"You're right," said Sam. "It's just the way we've done things in the past."

"It is a new day, Sam," I replied. "I believe you would have more loyalty and have more accomplished players wanting to play for the symphony if we had the reputation of taking care of our players."

"I suppose I could ask the Smiths to sponsor the musicians," Sam said. "They love seeing their names on things to show their friends. They didn't donate anything for auction, so I can leverage that."

I told Sam how much I needed to pay the musicians.

"That sounds reasonable," he said.

"Great. I can have the Clayton Quartet play. They said they were available."

"Wait, you already had them set up for the event?" Sam squinted at me.

"Of course, and I told them to pencil it in. If I couldn't get them any money, I wasn't going to ask them to play."

"Wow, Jerry, you have become ruthless," Sam chuckled.

"No, not ruthless. I'm looking after the musicians, who are the greatest asset to this organization. Without them, there would be no symphony. As a musician, I have felt a bit marginalized over the years. I want the musicians to know they are appreciated and will be paid what they are worth."

"I understand. No worries, mate," said Sam. "And you're right. I really appreciate you representing them. I believe some people on the board don't quite understand the hard work the musicians put in."

"It's not only the time and effort; our instruments are expensive. I could be riding in a nice Benz for what one of my basses cost."

Sam's brows went up. "Really?"

"Yes, really, and I don't have the most expensive instrument in the orchestra."

"I had no idea," said Sam.

"Well, I appreciate your support and understanding in this," I said.

I left Sam's office feeling good. I was worried I would get more resistance, but I knew that I had to try. Changing the culture of the company and shifting its goals and priorities would be a long process.

★ ★ ★

As I entered the door, Laura was sitting at the kitchen table. She had a serious look on her face.

"Hey, everything okay?" I asked.

"We need to talk," she said. "The kids are at a birthday party at Jackie's house."

I vaguely remembered that our friend Jackie's son Conner was having a party this week. It had completely slipped my mind.

"Oh, no, did I forget to take them?" I asked as I sat down.

"No, I had it handled, but I thought since they were gone, we could talk."

I was both hopeful and worried that we could talk about our relationship and how things had been going. We had tried a few sessions of marriage counseling, but Laura wouldn't open up, so we stopped going.

"I want to get right to it, Jerry. Since your accident, it has been really hard on me. We were having a tough time before then, but now it's becoming unbearable."

"I don't understand," I said in shock.

"We had a decent life a year ago, and I was hopeful that maybe you would audition for a bigger symphony or maybe start teaching over at one of the universities. We have been barely making it for some time. You promised that if I stayed home, you could pick up the slack, but things have only gotten worse, especially since you took on that new position."

I didn't want to lose my temper, and I wanted to listen to her, but so far she was saying that everything was my fault.

"I don't know why you're pursuing it like you are. Sure, you are making some more money, but you aren't a businessman; you are a musician. Why couldn't you just stick to that?"

"Do you want me to answer that?" I asked.

"Sure, because for the life of me, I don't understand," she replied.

"I have spent years, well beyond college years, learning my craft. I am a good bass player. Not a great one, but a really good one. But I am not a one-dimensional person. I have other interests and skills that I'd like to explore. Not only for the money aspect but because I am enjoying the process."

"Then why didn't you become a businessperson in college rather than a musician?"

"That is the tricky part. I was interested in business, and that is how I met Dr. Richardson. I took a few of his classes and loved them. The problem was that my music major took up much of my time. It wasn't just the classes – I had rehearsals for multiple ensembles, masterclasses, and lessons. There was little time for anything else. But I do regret not taking more business classes because, even as a musician, they were helpful. I have had to figure out a lot of things the hard way. I'm not the only one. Many musicians struggle, even ones with masters' and PhDs. Not only are the jobs scarce, but we are not taught how to make money or develop any other skills. It's not as easy as walking into a university and getting a tenured position in the music department."

"But did you even try?" Laura asked.

"Of course, I looked into it. I could give lessons, but I would be making a lot less money than I am now, and that is not a steady income."

Laura just frowned.

"Listen, the stuff I'm learning about project management could start a whole new career for me. I am learning fast and making a difference."

"A difference to who? I want a different life, Jerry. One in which I don't have to worry about money and where my husband pays more attention to me."

"I try to spend time with you, but lately you are gone. Mostly out with your friends," I countered.

"You just don't understand me. My friends get me. They like to have fun and go do things. You are working all the time."

I wanted to point out the obvious flaw in her logic. She wanted me to make more money, but she wanted me to work less and be around more.

"I admit, I've been really busy lately. I am trying to learn new skills, but I am building processes, so next year it won't be so difficult."

"Next year?" Laura scoffed. "How about now?"

I didn't know what to say.

"Then there is your injury. You don't even know if you'll be able to play professionally anymore. You have a master's degree in music. You are a dissertation away from a PhD. You need to concentrate on your future."

"I already explained the issue. . . ."

Laura cut me off. "I hate to say this, but your injury . . . makes you even less fun to be around. I constantly have to do things for you because you can't.

"That's not fair. . . ."

"And now you've turned our children against me," she blurted.

"What?"

"Corey has become a mini version of you. All he wants to do is play music. He doesn't have time for me. And Linda . . . she hates me."

"She doesn't hate you," I replied.

"She does. You have turned her against me. She is constantly telling me that I am wrong for arguing with you. She takes your side."

"I never told her to hate you. I can talk to her. . . ."

"What, so you can tell her that I'm nagging you?"

"Of course I wouldn't say that," I offered.

"Jerry, there's no point in arguing about this. I have decided that we need a break until you can get your priorities straight," Laura said.

It felt like a hard blow to the gut.

"You're leaving?"

"Yes. Jackie said I could stay with her until I found an apartment."

"But . . . what about the kids?"

"I'll help you get them to where they need to go, but they should stay here, so their school and life aren't interrupted too much. Besides, they adore you anyway."

"Can't we talk about this?" I asked.

Laura stood up.

"We have talked about it enough. I've made my mind up. I don't know what this will mean long-term, but for right now, I feel that it is the best."

My throat tightened. I was upset and angry, and my heart was torn out all at once.

I continued to sit at the empty table as Laura's car pulled out of the driveway. I was numb. What just happened?

I knew we had troubles, but I didn't think she would want a separation while we were trying to work things out. What was I going to do?

★ ★ ★

The next morning, I showed up for coffee with Dr. Richardson. Laura had dropped the kids back home, and after she tucked them in, she left again. In the morning, she arrived before they got up and made breakfast, and got them off to school. She said nothing as she got into her car and left again.

I wasn't clear what the kids knew and didn't know. They didn't seem upset, so I felt their mother hadn't told them yet. I guess over dinner I needed to have that conversation with them.

All of this was going through my head when Dr. Richardson sat down with his coffee and folder of papers.

"Are you all right, Jerry?" he asked in a concerned voice.

"Yeah, I didn't get much sleep last night."

"What's going on?" he asked.

I hesitated a moment before answering. We had become friends over the past few weeks, but I had not discussed my personal troubles. To be honest, I was a little embarrassed about it. But sitting here now, I felt like I needed to share what I was going through with someone. I didn't have a ton of close friends, mostly because I was an introvert, and most of the people I saw socially were Laura's friends as well. I definitely didn't want to pull them into my mess.

"Well . . . my wife left me last night," I said suddenly.

"What?" Dr. Richardson's eyes grew wide. "I am so sorry to hear that."

"With all the changes lately – my new job, my injury – I guess she isn't handling it all too well."

"The injury was an accident, and the job you are doing so well at," responded Dr. Richardson.

"Yeah, but she really doesn't want me to be the personnel manager. She wants me to teach," I said.

"But you are really good at your new position, and I'm not just saying that. You're flying through material that takes many students a whole semester to learn, and you're picking it up in days and weeks rather than months. I believe you're making a difference at the symphony."

"I tried to explain that, but she had made up her mind," I replied.

"Do you think it would help if I gave her a call?" Dr. Richardson said.

"Oh, no. I feel funny even sharing this with you," I said. "I feel like I'm imposing. . . ."

"Nonsense," Dr. Richardson said. "Your family's mental and emotional well-being is extremely important, not only to your quality of life but also to your job. It's hard to concentrate on work if the rest of your life is falling apart."

"True . . . but for now, I want to keep moving forward. If I sit and do nothing but feel sorry for myself, that won't benefit me or anyone else."

"Well, we can cancel today if we need to," Dr. Richardson offered.

"No, I really need the distraction right now. I feel she just needs to figure out what she wants, and as I am successful at my new job, I hope she can see how it will be a good thing for all of us."

"I hope so, too," Dr. Richardson replied.

I explained to him my discussion with Sam, and Dr. Richardson nodded and smiled.

"That's a great story," he said. "You're really digging into the core values of the organization."

"Yeah. I'm not sure someone in my position has done that before."

"Well, you're doing an excellent job," Dr. Richardson replied. "I think you will enjoy what we're going to talk about today: performance. Specifically, portfolio performance management."

He placed his stack of papers in front of me, and for the moment the knot in my gut that had been there all morning loosened a little. We started by revisiting the portfolio management process group chart. (See Figure 7.1.)

"In performance management, the process groups," Dr. Richardson began, "we're tracking basically three processes: develop a portfolio

Knowledge Area	Defining Process Group	Aligning Process Group	Authoring and Controlling Process Group
Portfolio Strategic Management	4.1 Develop Portfolio Strategic Plan 4.2 Develop Portfolio Charter 4.3 Define Portfolio Roadmap	4.4 Manage Strategic Change	
Portfolio Governance	5.1 Develop Portfolio Management Plan 5.2 Define Portfolio	5.3 Optimize Portfolio	5.4 Authorize Portfolio 5.5 Provide Portfolio Oversight
Portfolio Performance Management	6.1 Develop Portfolio Performance Management Plan	6.2 Manage Supply and Demand 6.3 Manage Portfolio Value	
Portfolio Communication Management	7.1 Develop Portfolio Communication Management Plan	7.2 Manage Portfolio Information	
Portfolio Risk Management	8.1 Develop Portfolio Risk Management Plan	8.2 Manage Portfolio Risk	

Figure 7.1 Portfolio management process group.

performance management plan, which is part of the project portfolio management plan; manage supply and demand; and manage the portfolio value.

"When we look at the mind map, we're basically looking at the process groups for developing portfolio performance management plan, managing supply and demand, and managing portfolio value. We're looking at all of the inputs, tools and techniques, and outputs." (See Figure 7.2.)

"This is like the other ones," I responded.

"Exactly," he replied. "According to the *Standard for Portfolio Management* by the Project Manager Institute, portfolio performance management is the systematic planning, measuring, and monitoring of

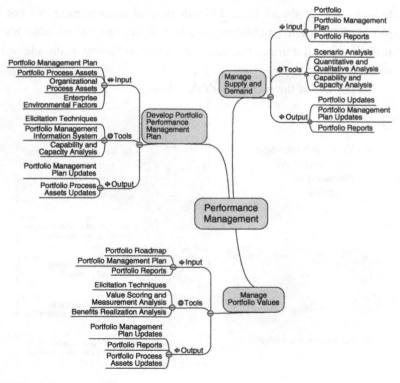

Figure 7.2   Performance management mind map.

the portfolio's value, organizational value, through achievement against the organization's strategic goals. Basically, we're measuring how we are performing against the strategic goals. We're not looking at performance from the standpoint of on time, on budget, or on schedule, as a project manager would. We're actually looking at the performance of how the portfolio is performing against being aligned to the strategic goals."

"I understand," I said.

He placed another page in front of me. (See Figure 7.3.)

"You've learned that to measure the project portfolio, you have to have the business drivers, which highlight and define what those business goals are. Then you're going to have KPIs or strategic impact statements that are going to give even further detail. How are we performing against those? It's a different type of measurement. It's not just metrics on time, on budget, on schedule, or even earned value. It's really looking at it from a business perspective, and are we really adding value to the business?

He pointed at the picture with the plane.

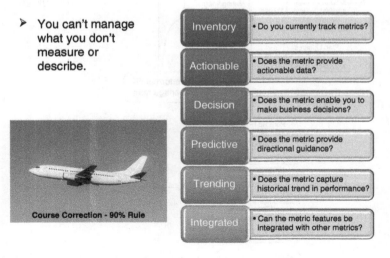

> You can't manage what you don't measure or describe.

Course Correction - 90% Rule

Inventory	• Do you currently track metrics?
Actionable	• Does the metric provide actionable data?
Decision	• Does the metric enable you to make business decisions?
Predictive	• Does the metric provide directional guidance?
Trending	• Does the metric capture historical trend in performance?
Integrated	• Can the metric features be integrated with other metrics?

Figure 7.3   Implementing performance management.
Credit: Media_Works/Adobe Stock Photos

"Did you know that whenever you fly somewhere, the aircraft that you're flying in is off-track ninety percent of the time?"

"No, I didn't. But that makes sense," I replied.

"Most of the trip, the plane is traveling in the wrong direction, even if it's just a few degrees off. Flying is not a straight line. The plane is constantly correcting its flight trajectory so that you end up in LA and not in Canada or in Mexico. The idea is that you can't manage what you don't measure or describe. The majority of the time, our portfolios are going to be off track. So we have to constantly have a process in which we can measure what's happening on a regular, consistent basis just like the computer on the plane, and constantly bring the portfolio back on the track."

"That makes me feel better because I feel like I've been building sandcastles on the shoreline. As soon as I build it up, the surf takes it down," I reply.

"That's a great analogy," said Dr. Richardson. "The focus is on the mission, and the mission is that we're targeting each department and making sure that we understand how to measure the metrics against them. We want to have a strategy with policies and processes, and procedures to focus on that mission and accomplish that mission. You have to have an objective. So you've been talking about getting the musicians more money. That has been your objective, right?"

"Yes."

"You saw another opportunity for that to happen – musicians playing at a fundraiser. You brought it back to Sam's attention that their main strategy was that the musicians needed to be paid a decent wage. That wasn't a part of your original project of getting them a raise, but it was your overall mission."

"Ah, I see what you mean," I replied.

"Metrics should follow a process," Dr. Richardson continued. "You should have an inventory of metrics that you're going to track, and those metrics should be actionable. In other words, when you see something that's going wrong, you can do something about it. You should be able to make decisions. The metrics should be predictive.

They also should have trending metrics, and you should also have metrics that are integrated so that they tell a holistic story about the performance of your portfolio."

"I made the decision to talk about paying the musicians with Sam because I saw that asking them to play for free was not in alignment with what we were trying to accomplish," I offered.

"You're getting it," he replied.

"Portfolio management performance has two types of metrics: tangible and intangible. Your tangible metrics are things that you can physically count, such as the increase in revenue, reduction in head-count or hardware costs, return on investments, a reduction of development costs, reduction in support of service maintenance costs, and reduction in facility costs. Those are things for which you can look in the bank account of the business and see the impact." (See Figure 7.4.)

"Like the pay increase for the musicians," I said.

"Yep!" replied Dr. Richardson. "The intangible metrics you need to track are strategic alignment. If you remember from the portfolio analysis view, there is an efficiency frontier view, but there's also a strategic alignment view to show how aligned to the portfolio is the current selection of projects to the prioritized business drivers that we get consensus from the executive team. Also, the degree to which we're mitigating risks – regulatory compliance, sustainability, optimization of human resources, and improvement in customer satisfaction. Many of these are squishy metrics, things that we really can't touch."

Tangible	Intangible
Increase revenue	Strategic alignment
Reduction in head count, hardware or software cost	Degree to which risks have been mitigated
Improved return on investment (ROI)	Regulatory compliance
Reduced development cost	Sustainability
Reduction in support or service maintenance cost	Optimization of human resources
Reduction in facilitate cost	Improve customer satisfaction

Figure 7.4   Portfolio management performance metrics.

"I get it," I said.

"When it comes to reporting portfolio performance, there are things that you can do around adding decision views, and some of the decision views are ways that you can look at the data. You can look at ROI, your internal rate of return, or net present value. You can look at the strategic impact. Again, that's an intangible one. You can look at the overall cost-benefit analysis of the portfolio itself and of the selected portfolio. You can have metrics where you can set up parameters to determine how much risk and how much opportunity each project has and then do some mathematics around that. Are you following me?"

"Yes," I said, making a lot of notes.

"Management views where you're looking at cost versus value. Also, when you can look at resource utilization, availability, capacity, and demand. Do you have any resource bottlenecks? In most organizations, there are few people who are the bottlenecks. Not that that's in a bad way, but what I mean by bottlenecks is that they have such a unique skill set that only maybe one or two people can do what they do, yet their skill set is in high demand, so they become a bottleneck to the business because the business can only go as fast as that resource can go."

"Fernando," I said.

"Fernando," Dr. Richardson repeated. "You either have to hire some additional people who can do what this person does and train them, or we have to figure out a way to streamline the work."

"But we can't do that with Fernando," I said.

"True, but some of the things you're asking him to do or need his approval on can be given to someone else. You said he doesn't like to deal with finances, so perhaps those choices should, in a formal way, be given to someone else. But think of this too. There are times that you have guest conductors, right?"

"Yes," I agreed.

"So there are others who can do his job. Perhaps he should have an assistant. Someone who can deal with getting you the numbers of musicians, ensure that the music is chosen, and other things that are essential to your job."

"Oh my gosh," I exclaimed. "You're right. And may God protect their soul as they work with him."

"It's just a suggestion, and it might not be in your budget, but it is something to consider," he replied. "Management also focuses on schedule, budget, and quality. Then you have operational views, whether it's processing activities, policies, or procedures. You can have metrics to cover all of those as well as your financial metrics. These are ways that you can begin to measure your tangible metrics as well as your intangible metrics."

"I like it," I said.

"In the performance management realm, we also focus on portfolio demand and supply," he continued. (See Figure 7.5.) "With supply, it's basically looking at resource capacity. What's the capacity of our team, the people, equipment, funding, information, or other assets? What about demand? What's the resource demand? When you look at all those coming through the pipeline, and you look at all the products that are happening, do you have a system in place that you can look

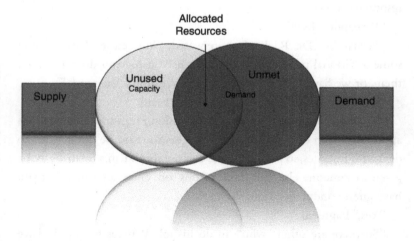

Figure 7.5 Portfolio demand and supply.

across and see the resource demand on those resources and if they have the capacity to handle that, as well as can the business or the customers handle all the change that you are producing?"

"Can you explain that a little further?" I asked.

"Resources should be allocated to minimize both unused capacity and unmet demand. In the area of portfolio performance management, portfolio change management falls within this area, and so in change management, we're looking at things like scope, requirements, scheduling, funding, as well as change, whether it's starting, stopping, or delaying, or reprioritizing a project. It's not changed from the standpoint of additional requirements for this project. That's managing the change that I just talked about earlier. But there's also change control, and it's at the portfolio level, so you have to remember that everything we're talking about is at the portfolio level. Change management is conducted within a controlled, structured environment, and it's facilitated by a change control board." (See Figure 7.6.)

"Yeah, I have trouble sometimes separating the portfolio aspects from the management parts," I admitted.

"That will come," he replied. "You are learning a ton of theory in a short amount of time. It will make more sense as you begin applying it to real-world situations."

"If you say so," I chuckled.

➤ Managing Change
   ✓ Scope
   ✓ Requirements
   ✓ Schedules
   ✓ Funding
➤ Change Control
   ✓ Starting
   ✓ Stopping
   ✓ Delaying
   ✓ Reprioritizing

Figure 7.6 Portfolio change management process.
Credit: Digital Storm / Adobe Stock

"The changing board is one of the boards that you would have as part of your governance process. The change control board is responsible for reviewing the impact the change will have on other portfolio components. After managing for a while, you can go to the change board. In your case, your board of directors, since you don't have a separate change board, but they act in that capacity. You'll come with your project and changes to the scope, schedule, or budget of your project."

"I have already done that," I said.

"Right. When you go and meet with them, you'll be looking at all of the projects. Is the change that they're requesting on one project having a ripple effect throughout their portfolio and does it cause issues? It also provides the purview to oversee, approve, reject, or reprioritize scheduling our resynchronization of any change requests. So again, we're not talking about change management from the standpoint of a single project. We're talking about change management at the portfolio level. It's a different mindset, skill set, and toolset."

"So when I bring them new ideas like, say, having more modern stands and stand lights, they would look at that in the larger context of it affecting other things such as the raise I have asked for the musicians."

"You're getting it," Dr. Richardson said, as he pointed at the next paper in the stack. (See Figure 7.7.)

"Another area of the project performance management is the portfolio management recalibration. The question to consider when you're thinking about portfolio recalibration is what is the best set of projects given the current budget and available resource capacity? Because the whole idea about calibration is that you're basically looking to reorganize or to take what you have and shake it up and look to see if you can optimize it anymore, especially if there are changes being introduced that could impact the portfolio or if there are external changes to the business environment that you have to consider, such as how to take care of a regulation and compliance project. How's that going to impact transforming the business project or growing the business project compared to our run-the-business project, which is just keeping the lights on in the business?"

➤ Tools required to recalibrate the Portfolio:
  ✓ Repriorized project list
  ✓ Efficient frontier
  ✓ Current resource allocation
  ✓ New project request
  ✓ Value/Cost bubble chart
  ✓ Value/Risk chart

➤ Recalibration Activities:
  ✓ Identify options to close execution gap
  ✓ Analyze multiple scenarios
  ✓ Define tradeoffs
  ✓ Select and approve portfolio changes
  ✓ Implement changes

Figure 7.7   Portfolio management recalibration.

I nodded.

"Something else we need to think about is whether you are getting the best from the projects in your portfolio. Are you getting the greatest return? Are they getting done quickly so that the business can receive the value that the project is going to deliver? Are you overinvesting in the portfolio? Because sometimes you can overinvest."

"Let's talk about the efficiency frontier. Organizations that use the efficiency frontier methodology are able to reduce waste and increase value creation by twenty to forty percent." (See Figure 7.8.)

"Wow," I exclaimed.

"The idea around efficiency frontier is where it says the optimal portfolio. A portfolio is optimal because the curve leading up to that portfolio is at its steepest. The trajectory is getting more bang for your buck. After that arrow where it says optimal, there's a little bit of bump-up. It's going up slowly but, from a risk standpoint and a cost standpoint, you're actually spending much more money to get that little bit of additional increase compared to the initial jump where you're at this arc up to the optimal portfolio. That's the idea of optimization.

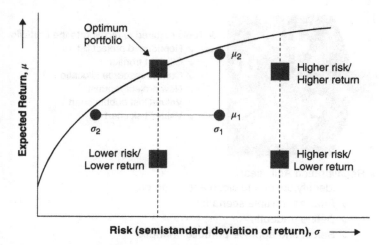

Figure 7.8 Portfolio efficiency frontier.

Should I invest additional funds for higher-risk and higher-return types of projects where I'm getting very little return on that additional investment, or should I keep the portfolio at this optimal portfolio area along the efficiency frontier curve?"

As I jotted down notes, I thought about the current projects in my portfolio and wondered what that optimum point would be.

"This is all based on algorithms, and there are systems that can do that," Dr. Richardson continued. "The main takeaway I want you to think about is an optimal portfolio that offers the highest expected return from a defined level of risk or the lowest risk for a given level of expected return. Portfolios that lie below the efficiency frontier are suboptimal. The ones that are way at the bottom, they're suboptimal."

"I hope my portfolio is not in those areas," I commented.

"I don't think it is, and besides, you're just starting out. This process is ongoing and one that you will need to monitor. If your port-folio falls into those suboptimal areas, you're not getting the greatest value for the money that you're spending because you don't have enough return for the level of risk. Portfolios that are at the right of the efficiency frontier are also suboptimal. In other words, the ones where it's a high risk, low return, high risk, high return because they have a high level of risk for a defined rate of return. The efficiency frontier allows you to understand the value that is destroyed by each constraint or by adding additional projects. That's why when you manage way too many projects, you may be killing your ability to gain value from those projects."

"Since you've had me prioritize my portfolio, I have significantly cut down the number of overlapping projects at one time," I said.

"Yes, and you will be thankful you did," he replied.

"Another way to manage portfolio management value is the portfolio variance report, the benefits realization plan, and the value scoring and measurements," he continued. (See Figure 7.9.) "According to

> Portfolio Variance Report

2004												
2005	0.0	0.0	0.0	0.0	0.0	0.0	0.0	0.0	0.0	6.1	-4.0	4.0	6.1
2006	6.7	-2.5	3.6	8.1	-1.2	-4.1	3.2	3.0	2.3	4.1	2.7	0.0
2007	0.8	-1.5	-1.4	3.7	2.4	-1.5	-1.5	-0.6	11.1	7.2	-2.3	5.7
2008	2.3	2.4	1.2	-0.8	3.4	2.7	-9.8	-5.5	1.5	-6.6	14.3	13.2
2009	-10.7	-0.2	-2.5	-2.3	9.5	-3.6	5.6	7.8	4.9	-3.6	2.0	3.9
2010	-5.4	5.4	9.8	6.4	-3.4	1.8	1.6	2.7	0.8	1.5	0.6	2.4
2011	-1.0	4.2	-3.5	4.6	-1.4	-2.6	5.8	12.3	-3.8	-1.4	-6.1	2.3
2012	2.2	-1.0	0.1	0.9	-1.8	1.4	3.3	-0.2	0.7	1.6	1.4	1.1
2013	-0.5	-1.3	4.3									

> Benefits Realization Plan

BENEFITS REALIZATION TABLE						
#	Description of Benefit	Tangible or Intangible	Who receives the benefit?	How is the benefit realized?	How will the realization of the benefit be assessed/measured?	Realization Date (MM/YY)
1						
2						
3						
4						
5						
6						
7						
8						

> Value Scoring and Measurement

Figure 7.9 Portfolio management value.
Credit: Minerva Studio / Adobe Stock

the *Standard for Portfolio Management*, the third edition from the Project Manager Institute, the portfolio value is defined as the aggregated value delivered by the portfolio components, and the components are projects, programs, and sub-portfolios. The goal is to deliver the maximum value possible aligned with strategic objectives and with an acceptable level of risk based on the risk tolerance of the organization. These are three types of reports that you can use to help you measure and manage your portfolio value. It's the portfolio variance report, the benefits realization plan, and the value scoring and measurement documentation."

As I looked at the next page (see Figure 7.10), Dr. Richardson said, "Here's some guidance on establishing portfolio manager reporting schedules and activities. Suppose you can pull the leadership team together to go through the reports on a monthly basis. You're looking for reports that are going to provide insight into past performance, and you're also going to look for reports that are going to provide forecasting of your expected results. In other words, those ones where it shows the portfolio value is optimized for the portfolio and is strategically aligned, or a cost versus value type of report. Also, you should include variance and variance analysis, its recommendations, and areas to be addressed. When you go to one of those, you should come prepared. It takes time for you to analyze the portfolio. When you're managing

> Review portfolio reports monthly

> Provide insights into past performance

> Provide a forecast of expected results

> Must include variance, variance analysis, and recommendations to address performance gaps

> Source of information for budget adjustments

Figure 7.10   Establish portfolio management reporting.
Credit: pressmaster / Adobe Stock

projects, your project reports are about how many hours did we use, are we on time, on budget, on schedule, are we under budget, are we meeting the requirements? Portfolio management requires a different set of skills."

"I'm beginning to understand that," I said.

"It's a different mindset. Now you're thinking about the variances of managing the overall portfolio, which is impacting the performance of the business."

"That is a lot," I said with a sigh.

"It is, but you are already doing some of this stuff from an instinctual level. I hope this will help you refine the process."

"It has been helpful," I said.

"Listen, I know this thing with your wife is weighing heavy on you," Dr. Richardson said as he placed a hand on my shoulder. "Pace yourself and take care of yourself. If you need to talk, please call me anytime. And I want to offer you again, if you need to pause our meetings for a while, we can."

"I think keeping as normal a life as possible will help me the most. I do appreciate everything, though."

"My pleasure," said Dr. Richardson as he left.

I sighed and scooped up my papers. It was time to go home and wait for the kids and the conversation I dreaded the most.

Dr. Richardson's Tips

- According to the *Standard for Portfolio Management* by the Project Manager Institute, portfolio performance management is the systematic planning, measuring, and monitoring of the portfolio's value, and organizational value, through achievement of the organization's strategic goals. Basically, we're measuring how we are performing against the strategic goals. We're not looking at performance from the standpoint of on time, on budget, or on schedule, as a project manager would. We're actually looking at the performance of how the portfolio is performing against being aligned to the strategic goals.

- Another area of the project performance management is the portfolio management recalibration. The question to consider when you're thinking about portfolio recalibration is: What is the best set of projects given the current budget and available resource capacity? Because the whole idea about calibration is you're basically looking to reorganize or to take what you have and shake it up and look to see if you can optimize it anymore.

- Another way to manage portfolio management value is the portfolio variance report, the benefits realization plan, and the value scoring and measurements. According to the *Standard for Portfolio Management*, the third edition from the Project Manager Institute, the portfolio value is defined as the aggregated value delivered by the portfolio components, and the components are projects, programs, and sub-portfolios. The goal is to deliver the maximum value possible aligned with strategic objectives and with an acceptable level of risk based on the risk tolerance of the organization.

CHAPTER 8

CHOOSING YOUR COMMUNICATION STRATEGY

The commissioned piece is late, and there is a worry that the completed parts will not be available to musicians before the first rehearsal. The conductor is unhappy and blames Jerry for not doing better. The composer is challenging to reach, and the answers to when music will be available are vague. But, because of the new music system, the parts are emailed five days before rehearsal. The piece adds two other parts, for a theremin player and a jazz saxophone player, and Jerry must scramble to find players. Neither player is someone that Jerry knows, and therefore he cannot assess if they are any good. In addition, they want twice the normal sub rate, and Jerry must get it approved two days before rehearsal.

Jerry and Laura try counseling. But after the third session, Laura doesn't show.

The kids are busy with activities at school. Corey makes honor orchestra at school. Jerry is doing lessons to make up for some of the shortfalls in income.

★ ★ ★

"Yes?" said Fernando in an irritated tone. I'd felt like I'd rather go through a root canal with anesthetic than have the conversation I was about to have.

"Do you have a minute to talk about *Toots Suite*?" I asked with a sense of embarrassment. It was such a silly name for a piece, and every time I had to discuss it with someone, I saw a Bugs Bunny cartoon in my head.

"What do you need?" Maestro asked. I was standing in the doorway, and I didn't feel invited in to sit in his office. It was fine because it gave me a quick exit should he decide to throw something at me.

"Well, I still don't have the parts, and when I try to reach KP Toots, he doesn't return my calls or emails."

"What would you like me to do about it?" Fernando replied. "You need to work this out with RJ. We have two weeks until we start rehearsals, and this simply is not acceptable."

"I am trying my best," I said.

"If this is your best, we are in trouble," said the maestro, as he scribbled on a conductor's score. "I can give him a call, but this is really your job."

I didn't know what else to say.

"Is there anything else?" he said, glaring at me.

I really didn't want to ask him any questions, but I needed to in order to do my job.

"Have you received your score for the piece? Do you know the instruments we need?"

He huffed and slammed down his pen.

"I got a piano score for it last week," Maestro snapped. "You should already know the instrumentation."

"I have the list I received from you a couple of months ago," I replied. "I have asked him if there are any changes, but I haven't received a reply."

"Then I believe it is safe to assume that it is the same," he said in a dismissive tone.

"Thank you," I said in a polite tone, even though I felt anything but polite. Maestro Fernando was just an abrasive person. I needed to figure out how to get on his good side or perhaps figure out a system in which I didn't need to come to see him in his office on a semi-regular basis.

* * *

Jerry, I am so sorry that I haven't gotten this to you sooner.
I am attaching pdfs of the parts. Below is the instrumentation.

4-4-4-4 3-2-3-3 3-4-4-1 3-timp
Alto sax
Theremin

Thanks,
KP Toots

I read the email a couple more times. A full string, woodwind, and brass section. That was prepared, but the last two instruments threw me into a fit.

"A theremin? Who uses a theremin?"

I remembered seeing a YouTube video of a woman singing with an electronic instrument that made a funny whining sound when a person moved their hand around it. It was mostly used in old horror movies to make spooky sounds. Was this guy serious?

First things first, I needed a saxophone player with two weeks' notice. I had only one person on my list.

"Hey, George, this is Jerry," I said.

"Hey, Jerry, how's it going?" said the voice on the phone.

"Okay, I suppose. Listen, I know this is last minute, but I need a sax player for October ninth's concert. Can you help us out?"

"I'm looking at my calendar," George said. "I can do the concert, but I know I can't do the last week of rehearsals because I'm doing a masterclass in Michigan."

My stomach dropped.

"Do you know anyone else?" I asked. "I looked at the part. It looks a little crazy. It's a commissioned piece."

"Hmm, I know a couple of guys, but I don't know how good they are. There is also Professor Lawson. He teaches trumpet at the university and plays in the philharmonic. But he may cost more."

"Just give me all their names and numbers. I'd appreciate it," I replied.

"I'll email them to you now. If you had asked sooner, I might have been more helpful," George said.

I was a little embarrassed by the situation. "I would have. I literally got the parts ten minutes ago."

"Bummer."

"I have another question, and I know this is nuts, but do you know anyone who plays the theremin?"

George laughed hard. "You mean that thingy you wave your hand and make that funky sound with?"

"Yes," I said in a defeated tone.

"No, man, I don't. Sounds like a wild piece. I hate that I can't play it. What's the name of it?"

"*Toots Suite.*"

"You're pulling my leg now." He laughed even harder.

"I wish I was. The composer is KP Toots."

"Oh man, that is too much. I definitely need to come to that concert."

As we hung up, I didn't feel as giddy as George sounded.

The first player I called said they couldn't do it. The next one sounded like a kid barely through puberty, although he was a freshman at the university. He could play it and was eager. I told him I would call him back. He was a warm body in the seat if I needed him, but I didn't think he could handle the part, and I would get quite an earful from Fernando about my incompetence.

"Dr. Lawson, thank you so much for returning my call," I said.

"No problem," he answered.

"I need a sax player for our October ninth concert. We have rehearsals Monday and Thursday the two weeks proceeding that and then a dress rehearsal on the ninth."

There was a pause. "I have one conflict on the seventh, but I can have one of my grad students cover that class, and then there is a church service on the ninth, but again I can get a sub for that. What does the gig pay?"

I told him our standard pay for subs.

"Oh, wow. I don't know. I'm going to have to pay my student to cover me, and I will be missing that gig. Can you do better than that?"

I was in a quandary. I could hire the other player for the regular rate, but he might not be able to play the part. If I increased the pay for Dr. Lawson, I'd have to get approval from Sam. Sam was going to be gone until next Tuesday, and I needed to fill the spot.

I give Dr. Lawson a different figure to consider.

"Sure, I can do it for that," he said cheerfully.

"Can I send you a pdf of the music?" I asked. "I can give you a hard copy when you come for the first rehearsal."

"A pdf will be fine."

"I have one other strange question," I added. "You don't happen to know a theremin player?"

Dr. Lawson chuckled. "Actually, Dr. Crepes plays it. Is there seriously a theremin part?"

"Yes," I said.

"I'll send you an introductory email," said Dr. Lawson.

"You're a lifesaver," I said.

* * *

On Tuesday morning, I met with Sam. He looked at the budget for the upcoming concert. I waited for it, and I saw his eyes go wide.

"What is a theremin? Is it made of gold?" he said in shock.

Between the theremin player and sax player, we had gone way over budget.

"I'm sorry, the KP Toots piece called for one," I said.

He signed off on the budget.

"I wish you had asked me first," Sam said.

"I thought about that," I replied. "Would it have made a difference? The piece was commissioned by the symphony, and that is what the composer decided to add. There might not be another theremin player in a two-hundred-mile radius, and if there was one, I wouldn't know how to find them. I had limited time."

"I guess you're right," admitted Sam.

"I think we should have a better process," I said. "Something that I can put online, and that you can see anytime, rather than waiting for you to come back to work. And perhaps a policy in which I don't need approval unless I need to go over budget by a certain amount."

Sam nodded. "That sounds like a great plan."

"I will set it up and send you an outline of what I'm proposing."

"I look forward to it," he said.

* * *

By the time I got home, I was pretty worked up. I went to another marriage therapy appointment, and Laura didn't come. She had been in and out of the house to help with the kids for the past month. Whenever I tried to talk to her, she never had time. I was still hopeful we could work some things out, but it was getting hard.

I opened the door, and Corey was jumping up and down. "Dad! Dad! I made it."

"Let me get in the door," I laughed. "What's going on."

"I made it into honor orchestra. My teacher says my lessons are paying off because I have improved a lot."

"That is fantastic news," I said and high-fived him with my good arm. "I think this deserves a pizza tonight!"

Linda was in the kitchen stirring a pot. "Sounds good to me," she said. "I can put this stew in the fridge for tomorrow."

I marveled at how mature Linda had become. She had taken on many of Linda's roles, and she rarely went out with her friends. While I appreciated her help, I felt guilty about all the responsibility she had to absorb.

"Why don't you go out with your friends this weekend? Go see a movie or something, my treat," I offered.

"I don't know, Dad. Don't you need me to help you clean this weekend? The living room is a mess," she replied.

"You don't worry about that. You already do enough," I said. "I really appreciate all you do, but you need to be a kid too!"

A smile brightened her face. "I'll text my friends now."

The kids didn't talk about it, but I knew they missed their mom. She was around, but only the required amount of time. She didn't take them anywhere, like for dinner or shopping. I was going to talk to her about it in therapy, but she hadn't shown up.

"Are we going for pizza?" prodded Corey.

"Yeah, yeah . . . get in the car, you two."

* * *

I had not seen Dr. Richardson in a few weeks. I had had to make some adjustments to my life. I was teaching some lessons from home in the evenings and on weekends to bring in a little more income. I asked Laura if she planned on working, and she acted as if she didn't hear me. She hadn't asked for money; she just used her credit card and debit card. It was another thing on our list to talk about. I cleared all that from my mind as Dr. Richardson sat down.

"How are things, my friend?" he asked.

"In some ways, better. The kids and I are getting into a routine now. I'm not sure where Laura and I stand right now, but I remain hopeful."

"I am sorry to hear that," he said.

"Don't worry," I replied. "I'm working through it."

"Tell me what I have missed since we last saw one another," said Dr. Richardson.

I brought him up to date on how my projects were going, and I emphasized what I did about the commissioned piece.

"Do you think I handled it okay?" I asked.

"I think you did more than okay. You assessed the project and ways you can improve in the future. Every time you do that, you are actually taking away some of the problems in the future. Great job."

"It's hard to sit firmly in my role and make big decisions. I am scared to make a mistake, but now I am more likely to just pick something and go with it rather than being paralyzed by what might go wrong."

"You are building your confidence, as you should. You are working hard to eliminate some of the risks by being direct and offering solutions."

"I appreciate you saying that," I replied. "Sometimes, when it's just me, I become unsure of myself."

"I recommend you think about building a network of other people you trust to bounce ideas off. They don't have to be in your industry, but they should have similar jobs and responsibilities as you do."

"That is a great idea," I said as I scribbled myself a note.

"Today, we are going to talk about communication strategy. It is timely considering what you went through this week," Dr. Richardson began. He slid a new stack of papers to me.

"Selecting a communication strategy is focused on satisfying the most important information needs of stakeholders so that every portfolio decision is made and organizational objectives are met according to the *Standard for Portfolio Management*." (See Figure 8.1.)

"The portfolio management process groups for communication management consist of two processes. And the defining process group is seen here. You develop a portfolio communication management plan, which is a part of the portfolio management plan. And then under the aligning process group, it's managing portfolio information." (See Figure 8.2.)

"The communication management plan and mind map have two processes," he continued. "They are the development portfolio communication management plan, which is a part of the portfolio management plan and manage portfolio information." (See Figure 8.3.)

"I'm following you," I said.

"When it comes to the communication management process overall, the first thing we want to do is the top box, which is the identification of stakeholder communication needs. So once we've done some form of an assessment or a questionnaire or just an interview process

Knowledge Area	Defining Process Group	Aligning Process Group	Authoring and Controlling Process Group
Portfolio Strategic Management	4.1 Develop Portfolio Strategic Plan 4.2 Develop Portfolio Charter 4.3 Define Portfolio Roadmap	4.4 Manage Strategic Change	
Portfolio Governance	5.1 Develop Portfolio Management Plan 5.2 Define Portfolio	5.3 Optimize Portfolio	5.4 Authorize Portfolio 5.5 Provide Portfolio Oversight
Portfolio Performance Management	6.1 Develop Portfolio Performance Management Plan	6.2 Manage Supply and Demand 6.3 Manage Portfolio Value	
Portfolio Communication Management	7.1 Develop Portfolio Communication Management Plan	7.2 Manage Portfolio Information	
Portfolio Risk Management	8.1 Develop Portfolio Risk Management Plan	8.2 Manage Portfolio Risk	

Figure 8.1   Portfolio management process group.

where we understand what the needs are, we also need to understand who are influencers and how interested they are and really just use all of the communication tools that we have. Then we want to develop a communication strategy and a matrix, and that matrix is going to help

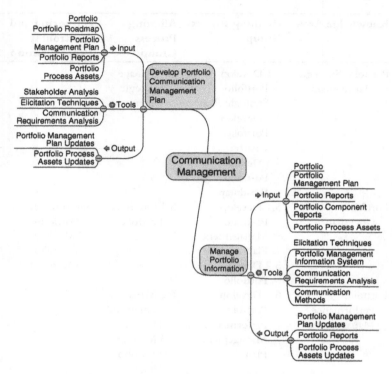

Figure 8.2 Communication management mind map.

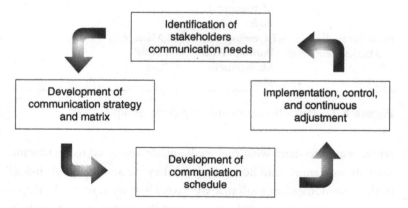

Figure 8.3 What is communication management?

us to identify who the most interested folks are. Who have the greatest interest? Who are our advocates? Who are neutral? Who are adversaries about the project or what we're doing? And we also want to understand that because we want to be able to manage folks at that level."

"I wish I could figure out a better communication with Fernando," I said.

"That will come, but I believe you are also building strategies in order to streamline your communications."

"This is true. I am motivated!" I said.

"We also want to understand the interest in the power grid based on if they have high power or low power. In other words, they can impact or influence the work that we're doing and just how interested they are. Because if they have high power and are very interested, they could derail our project or derail our portfolio. We want to understand exactly who is a part of our community as far as stakeholders and really manage them."

I nodded.

"I believe it will help to build communication with Fernando, Sam, and others. We want to develop it to understand what reports go out and when. What are our weekly reports? What are our quarterly reports? What are our monthly reports? Who gets those reports? Can some of those reports be automated from the system, or do all those reports have to be vetted? There are a number of things that we have to think through there. And then the implementation and control and continuous adjustment. And again, even in the communication strategy, it's like being on that plane where ninety percent may be off-target."

"I get that," I commented.

"You really want to focus on adjusting and figuring out who are your key stakeholders and really cater to them and help them to understand, teach. And show them so that as you communicate with them, they can help guard what you're doing and help you to be effective and move things along. Because if you have high-level executives who don't understand portfolio management and don't understand what you're bringing to the table, they can quickly derail your efforts."

"So get Sam and maybe some board members in alignment with me?" I asked.

"Exactly," Dr. Richardson replied. "When it comes to stakeholder expectations, their influence and interests, frequent and meaningful communication will keep them informed of steps along the way. You are mitigating the inevitable fears of change. Stakeholders who are aware of how the portfolio is progressing, how it will affect them, and the resources available to support them are more likely to support the portfolio, attend training, and use the new capability provided more effectively after deployment. So it's really important to communicate at the right level."

"Which is why Sam wanted to be more in the loop about last-minute budget changes," I said.

"You're getting it," Dr. Richardson agreed. "When I conducted the communication strategy and training at the law firm to introduce them to portfolio management, I went to New York to have a one-hour meeting with them to communicate and share. I tried to tie a lot of what I was bringing to the table into a lot of the jobs that they were already doing so they could easily relate to what we were talking about. The regular project managers had to be educated on portfolio management. Then we had the IT managers and functional managers on the business side. I had the project managers always communicate with them, and then we had to communicate with the regular team members. This was a situation where we were dealing with five countries and fourteen offices. And so you really do have to think through and be purposeful about your communication strategy and your communication execution."

I felt a little silly because I was dealing with only a handful of people in a small office. But then again, this was the perfect place to make mistakes because the stakes were lower. I was learning more every day, I felt, and perhaps one day I could take those skills to a larger organization.

"In regard to eliciting stakeholder requirements," Dr. Richardson continued (see Figure 8.4), "I remember sitting in a training while reading an article that talked about how Moscow is not only in Russia. And it made me scratch my head, and then I saw the acronym – MoSCoW stood for must, should, could, and won't; in other words, it means prioritizing your requirements. If something is a must-have, it's essential; if it's a should-have, it's important; if it's a could-have, it's nice to have; and a won't-have is out of scope."

"I have thought in those terms as I have prioritized my projects," I said.

"Yes, and it has helped, right?"

"Yeah . . . a lot."

"What you basically want to do is understand four things. First, who are your stakeholders you need to cater to with your communication strategy? Then what are their needs? Do they need hand-holding?

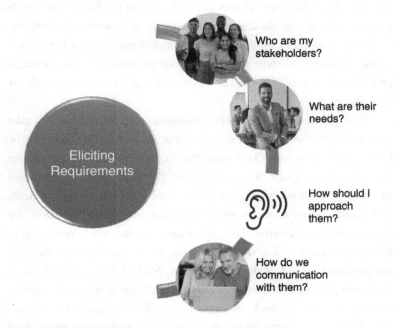

Figure 8.4   Eliciting stakeholder requirements.
Credits: Nicholas Felix/peopleimages.com/Adobe Stock; Lumos sp/Adobe Stock; nazar12/Adobe Stock Photos; Vadim Pastuh/Adobe Stock Photos

Do they need desk-side service? Do they need weekly reports? Do they need detailed, detailed, detailed reports? Do they need to see every project in the portfolio? Do they need to see the cost-benefit analysis and the benefits that are being promised for everything? Third, how should you approach them? And finally, how do you communicate with them in a way that they will accept and feel good about?

"You also have to look at the current culture, and you have to think about the fact that, when implementing any form of a portfolio management solution, you actually are changing the company culture to a great extent. And so, normally, when it comes to changing culture, companies struggle with that because you're changing people's behavior, and people don't want it. They want to grow, but they don't want to change."

"You have to help them grow and change by introducing them to incremental changes and trying to keep things as normal as possible as you introduce these new changes or new ways of working. That's really critical to be able to elicit solid requirements from your stakeholders."

I took a moment to study the slide and think about what he was saying. Incremental steps made sense, but sometimes I got impatient and wanted to push forward. It was something I needed to work on. (See Figure 8.5.)

"Your portfolio management communication strategy should take into account these five areas: awareness, understanding, acceptance, buy-in, and adoption. Over time, the higher you go up, the greater the amount of change you're asking for. When it comes to awareness of change, we need to provide them with the basic facts, key dates, and events. When it comes to an understanding of the intent of the change, we need to answer the questions of what the benefits are to the organization and what the benefits are to me. That's from their perspective. It's kind of the radio station, WIIFM: what's in it for me? And then gaining acceptance of the change. What is required of me to support the change? And what is required of the organization to support the change? These are the things that they're thinking about. And if you don't know the answers to these, then more than likely your

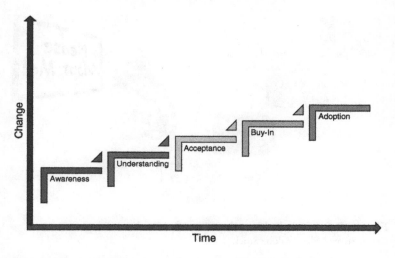

Figure 8.5 Portfolio management communication strategy.

communication plan will fail because they will derail it because they need to have these types of questions answered."

I took a lot of notes on the idea. I would look back over them and really contemplate what he was saying.

"In practicing change, you want to create buy-in. Buy-in is a team sport because you'd never see one individual winning the Super Bowl or the pennant or the NBA Finals. It's always a team effort. In some form or other, everyone has to accept the change, and they have to want to support the change for the best of the organization."

"I get it," I said in agreement.

"And lastly, adoption," he continued. (See Figure 8.6.) "What you really want is to create a group of advocates for the change so that they can help communicate and get other people on board. You want them to practice the change every day, and you want them to tell others about the great impact. And the great impact is going to happen when it impacts their lives personally. When they see a personal benefit in doing work this way, they will change. If they don't see a personal benefit to themselves – not to you, but to themselves across the board – they won't change. And the only way to really implement massive

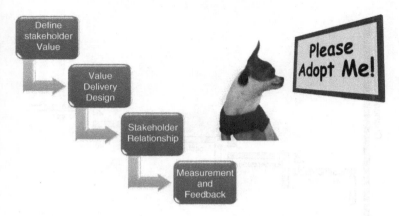

Figure 8.6   Stakeholder adoption of portfolio management.
Credit: Stuart Miles / Adobe Stock

change is that you have to communicate it in a way that everyone sees the benefit and it's specifically for them personally."

"I believe working closely with the board and the orchestra committee will help me better achieve that."

"I concur," said Dr. Richardson.

"When it comes to adoption, there are basically four steps. We want to define the stakeholder value, and we want to have the delivery design. In other words, we're going to figure out how we're going to deliver value. And then we want to have and understand the stakeholder relationships, and finally, we want to measure and get feedback. Ken Blanchard says, 'Feedback is the breakfast of champions.' So, to define stakeholder values, we want to identify stakeholders and assess their needs and expectations. Undervalue delivery design; we want to glean requirements, define the scope, and develop a communication management plan."

"Makes sense," I said.

"Under the stakeholder relationships, we want to analyze stakeholders, develop strategies to engage the stakeholders, and manage their expectations. And then, under measure and feedback, we want to provide information, monitor communication, and manage stakeholder engagement. We want them to adopt our system, but they also want to be adopted and feel like they are brought into the fold."

"Implementing project portfolio management should establish a culture, not just a system that enables a process for systematically aligning the organization's attitudes, behaviors, and actions, which should result in an interrelated and prioritized portfolio that yields better outcomes while minimizing the investment of the organization and resources. It is critical to think through the culture."

Dr. Richardson pointed at the paper in front of me. (See Figure 8.7.)

"I like this because there are two different companies and you can see by the physical environment that there are two totally different cultures. The one on the bottom looks like a law firm, and the one on

Figure 8.7   The power of culture.
Credit: Monkey Business / Adobe Stock

the top looks like an ad agency. The way they have meetings is totally different from what the top organization has compared to the way the bottom organization has. Is your organization formal? Is it a major law firm? Are they Ivy Leaguers? Is it a PR firm? Is it an IT shop? It depends whether you work at Amazon, Google, or Zappos, or you work at Saks Fifth Avenue."

"Or a symphony orchestra," I added.

"Yes, of course," Dr. Richardson chuckled. "It depends on where you work and the environment as you roll out project portfolio management. You have to understand the power of culture, because if you don't, it can derail your project. It can kill an effort; it can put it on the back burner because if it rubs up the wrong way against the culture, people will not stand for their culture to be denigrated. You have to embrace it and show them how to make those changes that you're trying to help them make."

I continued my note-taking.

"When it comes to the communication governance guidelines, here are some questions to consider. How will the communication plan be changed? Who is responsible for making changes to the plan? Who approves these changes? How will the person responsible for executing the communication item be notified, and how will communications be tracked?"

"I got," I said, as I finished writing.

"That's all I have for this week," Dr. Richardson said. "Is it helpful?"

"Enormously," I responded. "As always, I am extremely appreciative."

"I know at times you feel you are on the front lines alone," Dr. Richardson said. "I am a phone call away, and I do suggest creating or even joining a group of like-minded professionals."

"I am on it," I said, as I shook his hand.

As I headed home, I thought about my week. There were so many great things going on at work, and the kids seemed to be doing well. The issue of my relationship weighed heavily on me, and I felt helpless as to what I needed to do. Maybe I just needed to let go of the guilt and feeling responsible for everything. Perhaps I needed individual therapy in addition to marriage counseling.

Dr. Richardson's Tips

- Selecting a communication strategy is focused on satisfying the most important information needs of stakeholders so that every portfolio decision is made and organizational objectives are met according to the *Standard for Portfolio Management.*
- We also want to understand the interest in a power grid based on whether they have high power or low power. In other words, they can impact or influence the work that we're doing and just how interested they are. If they have high power and are very interested, they could derail our project or derail our portfolio. We want to understand exactly who is a part of our community as far as stakeholders are and really manage them.
- When it comes to adoption, there are basically four steps. We want to define the stakeholder value, and we want to have the delivery design. In other words, we're going to figure out how we're going to deliver value. And then we want to understand the stakeholder relationships, and finally, we want to measure and get feedback.

CHAPTER 9

CHOOSING YOUR RISKS STRATEGY

It struck without notice, without warning. A worldwide pandemic and everything changed in an instant. The kids were home, and Laura was missing in action. I didn't even know where she lived anymore. I knew better than to say that things couldn't become worse because I knew that was just begging for it.

I had to send out an email that I dreaded. Our next concert will be canceled. What was I going to do? In a couple of months, the holiday season would start, and every day I was getting notices that those gigs were being canceled. I knew I was not alone in my feeling that things were going to become worse – much worse. The musicians relied on these gigs to eat and pay bills.

Many musicians taught lessons, but how were they going to do that with social distancing? I was figuring this out myself, and fortunately, my students introduced me to video conferencing. It was not quite the same as being in person, so I needed to adjust my teaching style.

The next day I would have to meet with the board, Sam, and Fernando. I had terrible heartburn, worrying about my position being cut. I hoped to make the argument that they needed me more than ever. Fernando wouldn't care as long as it didn't impact his salary. Sam was more fiscally responsible, and so he was a wild card on which way he would land.

There was a lot on the agenda, and I knew that I wouldn't be sleeping much. Where was Laura when I needed her? I could have used some support, especially now that both kids were home, and were receiving their education through video conferencing. Was this the new normal – everyone communicating through a device, and people no longer interacting in person? For now, this would be the way of things, but I worried about how long and whether the symphony could weather this storm.

It wasn't about ticket sales because these were not what paid the bills. It was sponsorships, trusts, and contributions that were the lifeblood of the symphony. People supported the symphony through their generosity, but what would happen if there were no live concerts? Would people continue being generous?

I watched my symphony friends on social media in absolute panic, and my heart went out to them. What could I do to help? I had a list of ideas that I would present to the board, but I was unsure if they would endorse them because of the risk involved at such a chaotic time. My core mission was to serve the musicians and the symphony. I needed to provide lifeboats for a sinking ship.

"Hey, Dad," said Corey, "I brought in the mail."

Corey was looking for anything to do to break the monotony of being trapped in the house all day. Neither of the kids had been able to see their friends and spent most of their off-school time online chatting. It made for a tense time, but they were adapting the best they could.

Laura had not visited in the past couple of weeks, saying she was afraid to bring the virus to the kids. I told her that they weren't going out, and so if everyone gave each other space and wore masks, they should be okay. She wouldn't hear of it and went radio silent with me. The kids said they got texts from her most days asking how they were, but not more than that.

I flipped through the mail and stopped at a letter from Conner & Conner, Attorneys at Law. My stomach dropped. My name and address were handwritten, and that didn't bode well. This wasn't an advertisement; this was official. The other clue was the "Confidential" stamp on the front and back.

In my heart, I knew what it was, but I felt like if I just ignored it, it wouldn't be true. I stood frozen in the kitchen, letter in hand. Linda walked in and stopped.

"Dad? Are you okay?" Her voice was in panic mode.

"Yeah . . . yeah," I replied, snapping out of my shocked state.

"Are you sure? You're not having a heart attack or something, are you?"

"Of course not," I replied, feigning a smile.

"You looked like you were in pain . . . a lot of pain," Linda said.

"I'm just tired, I guess," I said. "I have that meeting tomorrow with the board, and I'm nervous."

"Dad, you will be just fine," she said. "You got this."

I smiled in earnest.

"Where did a daughter like you come from?" I said, and embraced her.

"You're lucky, very lucky," replied Linda with a smile as she squeezed me hard.

"Do you mind if I order pizza tonight?" I asked. "I don't have it in me to cook."

"Pizza . . . oh no, that," she said dramatically with her hand strewn across her brow.

I laughed. "Okay, okay. You guys order, okay? You know what I like. I'll be in my office working for a bit."

Linda ran off screaming, "Corey . . . Dad is being abusive again and letting us order pizza. What do you want? Remember, pineapple is not a real topping."

As I retired to my office and closed the door, I took a moment to be thankful. It might be a pandemic, and the world was upside down, but I was blessed with two wonderful, beautiful children. No matter what happened next, I would always have that.

★ ★ ★

"Are you kidding me?" I said to Laura on the phone. My blood pressure was through the roof. I was furious.

"Don't raise your voice at me," she replied.

"You say nothing, and then you have an attorney send this ridiculous separation agreement."

"Does this surprise you?" she asked.

"In some ways, it does, but the part about the kids living with you and me paying you to support . . . is ridiculous. You left and have provided no support. You haven't seen the kids in weeks, and even before this pandemic, you saw them only a few times a week."

"Children belong with their mother," she said flatly.

"I'd love for you to spend all the time you want, but having them live with you and pay you money . . ." I said more loudly than I wanted. I tried to take a couple of breaths and regain my composure. "I have been supporting them solely. You continue to use the credit cards and bank account at your leisure."

"Listen, my attorney has advised me not to even talk to you right now," she replied.

"Where are you even living? Do you even have room for them? They don't want to move schools. You don't even have a job or any income that I know of."

"They will have plenty of room, and Jim makes plenty of money. He has no problem with the kids staying with me. He has a great job, so he can take care of us. You just need to pay support and take care of your responsibility."

I felt something break inside me.

"Jim? Who the hell is Jim?"

"That is not really any of your business," Laura replied. "Come on, Jerry, you knew it was over. Did you expect me to remain alone?"

"We aren't divorced," I snapped back. "How long has this been going on? I thought we were working on things."

"You may be working on things, but I am done. I have been done for quite some time. Jim takes care of my needs in a way you never could."

I felt she was just baiting me now. "Have you talked to the kids about any of this?" I asked.

There was a long pause on the phone.

"Are you still there?"

"I was thinking it best for you to prepare them. I want to pick them up Friday, so I'd appreciate it if you had their things ready.

I know you are a little short on money, so you can start paying support next month."

I couldn't take it anymore.

"Laura, I will not be preparing them for anything. If you wish to tell them you are living with some guy and want them to live with you, you do it. But know this, I will also be getting an attorney. I don't believe for a moment that pulling the kids from their home because you want to start a new life is in their best interest."

Laura laughed. She actually laughed.

"You actually want to fight me in court? Really? With what money? You barely make enough following that stupid dream of being a manager or whatever you're doing. You might have had a chance as a musician, but that's over now that you injured yourself. Don't drag the kids through a nasty court battle that you have no chance of winning. Jim Conner is one of the best litigators in town."

"You are sleeping with your attorney?" It was my turn to laugh. "You are really something, Laura. After all these years, I don't believe I have known you at all. You're welcome to visit the kids or call, but I'm not letting you leave with them. We will let a judge decide on that."

I hung up the phone before she would respond. Nothing further could be said that would be productive. I kicked the wastebasket.

"Man," I exclaimed, and the basket crashed into a lamp.

"Dad?" said Linda as she rushed into the room. "What happened?"

As I looked at my daughter, I knew I would be willing to fight for her and her brother. But I didn't want my hurt pride to decide their future.

"You and your brother need to come in here," I sighed.

★★★

Morning came swiftly. I calculated I might have slept three hours tops. I really wanted to cancel the call today, but I couldn't. I needed to push aside the Laura stuff from my mind for the time being. I needed rest and perspective. I also needed an attorney and had no idea how I was going to afford that.

The kids took the news better than I would have ever imagined.

"Dad, we're going to stay with you," answered Linda, and Corey nodded with tears in his eyes. "I think Mom has lost her mind. I'm not going anywhere."

"Are you sure?" I asked. "I don't want to get into a battle with your mom unless I need to. If you think you'd be better off over there, then I'm not going to stand in the way of that."

"No one is going to make me move. This is my home, and you take great care of us."

Both Linda and Corey grabbed me. Tears stained my shirt, and I was not sure if they were mine or theirs. Why did Laura have to do this?

I had a half-hour before my call. I shaved and downed a cup of coffee. The one benefit of these calls was that all I needed was a dress shirt. I could wear sweat pants and slippers if I wanted.

People appeared on the call one by one. They went through some business matters that didn't involve me, although I listened carefully. Then the floor was turned over to Sam.

"As you all know, it was with much regret we had to cancel our next concert," he said. "I feel this is just the beginning. So we need to make some decisions about how to move forward the next few months."

"I don't understand why we couldn't have the concert," interrupted Fernando. "We will be onstage away from the audience. They can wear masks."

"I believe that the situation is more complicated than that," replied Sam. "The musicians need to be protected from one another. Sure, the string players could wear masks, but what about the wind and brass players?"

Fernando made a face like he had swallowed a bug.

"Besides, the government is setting stricter guidelines every day. We wouldn't be able to have the concert if we wanted to. In addition, people are afraid right now. They wouldn't come out anyway," replied Sam.

Various concerns on both sides of the issue were batted around.

"We need to discuss the quartet," said Sam. "I don't believe they will be able to finish out their concert series this year. There is talk of closing the borders, and they want to go home. We can pay out their contract."

"What?" shouted Fernando. "No, you can't send them home. They are my strongest players in the symphony. I picked pieces for the rest of the season. Where are we going to get musicians of their caliber when all this blows over? Do you think you could find players good enough, Jerry?"

"Well, I . . ."

"Exactly," Fernando cut me off. "It's settled. They stay."

"Again, it is not that simple. If they aren't working, then it can affect their visas. We can talk about bringing them back next year when all of this is over," replied Sam.

"What about the other musicians? Are you going to pay their wages for the season too?" Fernando asked.

"We are trying to work on a plan for that," he replied.

"So the answer is no," Fernando returned.

"I didn't say that; we just need to figure out what that looks like," Sam said. "Jerry and I can review the numbers and see what makes the most sense."

"I understand the board's concern about paying the musicians if they aren't performing," I jumped in. "But they have families and bills too. My understanding is that ticket sales don't pay for the concerts. Our costs in the next few months will be reduced. We don't have to pay for music or rent the hall, which are two of our largest expenses. We could pay the musicians for at least the upcoming concert. It would be unfair not to, as they count on that money. We can look at each upcoming concert and make decisions as they come up based upon what is happening."

I saw a lot of nods, including Fernando. I released a breath I didn't know that I was holding.

"I know that you have been nervous about us cutting your position," said Sam. "Before we got on the call, we decided to keep you on for the season, as we have that in the budget. After that, we are not sure."

"What he is trying to say," said Fernando with a sneer, "is that he is not sure there will be a symphony after this season."

***

After the call, I wanted to drink . . . a lot. At least my job was secure, but I needed to be creative to help the musicians to make sure that the symphony was taking care of them.

I quickly typed an email to let everyone know they would be paid for the canceled concert and that we were working on what the rest of the season would look like. I knew this would be a relief to many of them.

My call with Dr. Richardson was starting in a few minutes. I was relieved that he agreed to meet with me virtually.

"Can you hear me?" I asked when Dr. Richardson's face appeared on the screen.

"Yes, can you hear me?" he responded.

"Loud and clear. Thank you so much for meeting with me this way."

"It's no problem," he said. "I have had to meet with my students this way, so I learned how to use the software quickly. What a world we are living in."

"You're telling me," I chuckled.

"Before we begin, I hate to pry, but I wanted to ask you how things were going with your wife and kids."

A lump formed in my throat. I thought I was going to cry. I couldn't do that.

"I . . . well . . ." I stammered.

"Oh, Jerry, I didn't mean to upset you."

"No, no . . . you're fine," I said. Dr. Richardson and I had become more than mentor and student in the past few months. We had become friends, and I needed a friend about now. I unloaded the burden of my wife's desire to take my kids away and the fact I felt helpless to stop it.

"Hmm," he said. "You are a good man and a good father. I don't usually get involved in others' affairs, but you are a dear friend. I am going to introduce you to an attorney friend of mine. He owes me favors and a few debts from losing to me at golf. I feel confident he will help you and work out a financial arrangement that you can handle."

A tear escaped my eye. I couldn't stop it.

"I don't know what to say . . . thank you." It felt so inadequate.

"My pleasure, Jerry," he replied. "Are you ready to dig in today?"

"I am now," I said as I wiped away my tears.

"This is an unsure time for your symphony, and so they will need to do business differently. That means they are taking on a lot of risks. So I hope today's lesson will help you. I will send you these slides at the end of our call."

"Perfect," I replied.

"Measuring risks is a part of the project portfolio management function both at the project initiation and throughout the life cycle of a project portfolio," he began. "We've made it to the portfolio management process group for risk management. And in this process group, you have two processes – develop the portfolio risk management plan and manage the portfolio risk." (See Figure 9.1.)

"I see," I replied.

"We have inputs, tools, and outputs," he continued. (See Figure 9.2.) "You want to really study these mind maps and understand the various inputs to the process, the tools and techniques, and the outputs."

I made myself some notes.

"Risk management is the cumulative effect of the probability of uncertain occurrences on certain events that may positively or negatively affect project objectives or the portfolio, and risk can be positive or negative," he said. "Think of a company that advertises its systems and new services on the web during the Super Bowl to over a hundred million people. Those watching log in, and their servers crash. That's a positive risk."

"I think I understand," I said.

"They got a positive result, but they weren't prepared for that positive result. It seemed like it turned out negative, but if they had considered it

Knowledge Area	Defining Process Group	Aligning Process Group	Authoring and Controlling Process Group
Portfolio Strategic Management	4.1 Develop Portfolio Strategic Plan 4.2 Develop Portfolio Charter 4.3 Define Portfolio Roadmap	4.4 Manage Strategic Change	
Portfolio Governance	5.1 Develop Portfolio Management Plan 5.2 Define Portfolio	5.3 Optimize Portfolio	5.4 Authorize Portfolio 5.5 Provide Portfolio Oversight
Portfolio Performance Management	6.1 Develop Portfolio Performance Management Plan	6.2 Manage Supply and Demand 6.3 Manage Portfolio Value	
Portfolio Communication Management	7.1 Develop Portfolio Communication Management Plan	7.2 Manage Portfolio Information	
Portfolio Risk Management	8.1 Develop Portfolio Risk Management Plan	8.2 Manage Portfolio Risk	

Figure 9.1   Portfolio management process group.

as a positive risk, they would have thought through that they needed a more robust platform to handle all of the millions of requests."

"Oh, I get it."

"Portfolio risk management is about the processes involved in identifying, analyzing, and responding to project and portfolio risk consisting of risk identification, risk quantification, risk response development, and risk response control. That's a mouthful, I know."

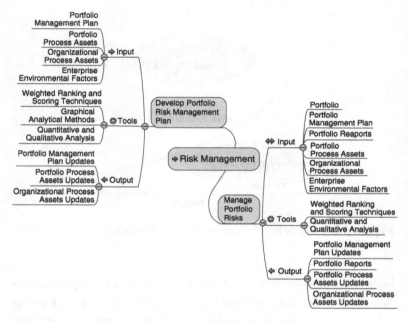

Figure 9.2 Risk management mind map.

"I'm following you," I replied.

"One of the ways to manage portfolio risk is to understand the risk tolerance of the organization and of your portfolio office. So as you look at the chart here, you see that you have probability and impact. This is important right now. You need to determine how much risk the symphony can take, considering the pressure it's under. Do you let some projects go for now? What about new ones?" (See Figure 9.3.)

"I have considered that very thing," I admitted.

"If you have a project that has a high probability of happening and high impact, if you're using something along this line, when you're managing your risk and communicating with your executives, you can help them see that that is a risk that you can't take on or that you need to work around or you need to really focus on developing a mitigation strategy to address that risk, so it does not happen," Dr. Richardson explained. "There are varying different types of risk tolerance. There's

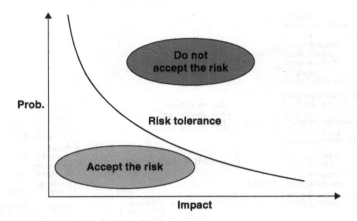

Figure 9.3   Portfolio management risk tolerance.

high risk tolerance and a high tolerance for business opportunities. When it's a high tolerance for business opportunities, we encourage creativity and some experimentation. In other words, we welcome that marketing of a system at the Super Bowl with potentially one hundred million people coming and hitting the server so that we can be creative and bring in a lot more money to the company."

"The medium level two is operational threats. Now with operational threats, we are addressed to ensure continuity and success. In other words, you want to make sure you have a strong disaster recovery plan. Under medium one tolerance, which is strategic threats, it can lead to a crisis. This is a probability that's high, and the impact may be moderate, but it's in an area of the business that could create a strategic threat to the business even being around the next day."

I studied the slide that he was talking about and thought about the current crisis we were in and reprioritizing our projects.

"And then low tolerance, which is a strategic crisis, is a danger of coming to a halt. In other words, if you have low tolerance, something is in a strategic crisis. If you have a high tolerance, you can handle a lot of the heavy risks, but if you have low tolerance, you can't."

"I believe we are at a low tolerance due to not being able to have concerts and having to send our best players back to their home countries. We need lower-risk plans," I offered.

"I one hundred percent agree," Dr. Richardson said. "This is another way of looking at it. If you've ever done a risk assessment where you've listed out your risk, and you calculate it, red, yellow, green probability and probability and impact. Or if you had used the mathematical formula in an Excel spreadsheet to calculate your risk, or you have a risk system, or you do a Monte Carlo simulation, which is used to determine the probability of an outcome based on random sampling many permutations to show you what's the probability of that risk. This is one way to be able to communicate to your leadership team about the level of risk tolerance and understanding their risks tolerance."

Dr. Richardson continued (see Figure 9.4), "Now with the risk rating for likelihood and impact or probability and impact, you could actually lay the previous chart on top of the risk rating chart, and you can see that the areas where it would have been low tolerance, or tolerance that risks are acceptable, would be in the green area.

Figure 9.4   Risk rating.
Credit: wor_woot/Adobe Stock Photos

The likelihood that you have a high level of risk leads to the yellow or to the red area, which goes to the right and up in the corner. If a risk falls within that category, that is very likely to happen, and the impact would be critical. That could be a risk that the business just can't take on, and you have to come up with a strategy to manage that. That's what risk management is all about – it's really about problem prevention. Identifying potential problems before they occur. Analyzing those problems, figuring out a solution for those problems."

"This is exactly what I need right now," I said.

"Here's an example of a risk register that you can leverage. The ability to be able to manage risk or see risk across your portfolio can really help you develop a comprehensive approach to managing risk and keeping the portfolio moving forward as far as being able to optimally recalibrate it and adjust it so that you're using resources in the most optimal manner and you're keeping the costs down as well as delivering great value to the business." (See Figure 9.5.)

"I love it!" I said.

"You also want to assess the business or organizational requirements, the degree of any organizational risks that may happen and so, especially at the portfolio level, your risks are not just as it used to be as a project manager where you're looking at risks to the project,"

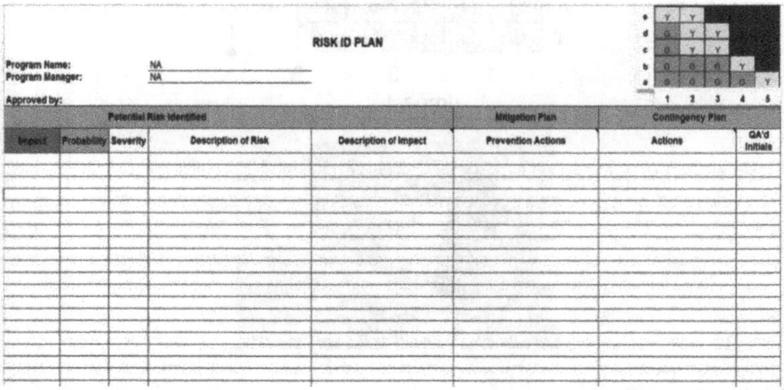
RISK ID PLAN

Program Name: NA
Program Manager: NA
Approved by:

Potential Risk Identified					Mitigation Plan	Contingency Plan	
Impact	Probability	Severity	Description of Risk	Description of Impact	Prevention Actions	Actions	QA'd Initials

Figure 9.5 Portfolio risk register.

Dr. Richardson continued. "You're actually looking at risk to a department, a risk to the business, a risk to a division, a risk to the entire organization, when you're thinking about portfolio level risk. Are you following me?"

"I am," I replied.

"Great, now I want to introduce you to a really neat tool called Pugh's risk strategy matrix. This matrix is used at the portfolio level or on major projects or programs. Let me just give you an example." (See Figure 9.6.)

"Pugh's risk matrix evaluates and prioritizes a list of options when you're thinking about a risk that you have to deal with. You can use this for a major risk. It's not for all of the risks at one time. It's for a major critical risk that can happen."

"I feel everything is a critical risk right now," I commented.

"The person who taught me this matrix, Carl Pritchard, gave it to me in a class that I took from him. He was talking about a company over in Europe that had work in the Congo in Africa. And the country was experiencing a unrest at the time. The project manager went to his boss and said, 'I just did my risk assessment, and for us to be effective on this project, we need a helicopter.' The gentleman looked at him with a questioning expression. 'You need a helicopter? Why?'

"Carl replied, 'Because the country's unstable and if something happens in the middle of the night, the roads are bad. We're not going to be able to get anybody out. We won't be able to get the equipment out, and we're going to end up losing a lot of our team members. They may even get killed, and so we need a helicopter.' Carl put together

Risk Strategies	Risk 1	Risk 2	Risk 3	Risk 4	Time	Cost
Risk Strategy 1	−	+	−	0	−	+
Risk Strategy 2	+	+	0	+	+	+
Risk Strategy 3	0	+	−	+	+	−
Risk Strategy 4	+	+	−	+	+	−
Risk Strategy 5	−	−	+	+	−	+

Figure 9.6 Pugh's risk strategy matrix.

a whole strategy around this, and he used Pugh's matrix to figure out that that was the best strategy for dealing with the risk. He started the project, and a few months in, they started hearing gunfire in the middle of the night. The gunfire started getting closer and closer. Luckily the company and executive team had thought about what he had said and had approved his use of helicopters in an emergency. They were able to quickly pack up their kit, take whatever they could, get into the helicopter, and fly away. Hundreds of people died from that firefight, but not those from his company."

"That's amazing," I said.

"The idea of using this is when you have a list of options that you have to narrow down to choose one. So let's say you have that risk of something really bad happening. You want to then look at the risk strategies and list the names of the risk strategies and the potential risks. For each one where the risk strategy has a positive impact, you want to put a plus sign. If it has a negative impact, you put a minus sign. If there's no impact, you put a zero. When it comes to time and cost, you want to put a positive sign or a cost sign. For costs, you want to put a positive or a negative sign as well. Then you can look across and look for the most positive attributes around how to handle that risk. So if you look at the sheet that we have there, risk strategy two, whatever that would be, whatever risks you're dealing with, it would be a better risk strategy that you want to address the first, second, and fourth risks. With time and costs, you have a positive sign, which says that risk strategy two, whatever it is that they've come up with, would address those areas."

"I need to use this when figuring out the compensation strategy for the musicians moving forward," I said.

"Another level of risk management is when you look at portfolio dependencies and interdependencies. Anytime you have projects that have dependencies on other projects, it's almost like integration of management in the theory of constraints world; when you have multiple lines coming together or multiple projects coming together to deliver a program, it's considered very risky," he said. "You will want to increase the amount of buffer that you have when you're planning those, doing that kind of planning. Anytime you have any kind of portfolio dependencies or multiple project dependencies or programs where projects have to deliver for others to be able to deliver, that creates an enormous risk."

This information was hitting close to home. I had created a number of projects that depended on one another, and now that the pandemic was upon us, some of those projects would be put on hold, but at the same time, it could affect others.

"Here is a quick story around the *Titanic*," Dr. Richardson said. "The *Titanic* had a sister ship called the *Olympic*. And during that time, there was a major decision made to redeploy some of the team from the *Titanic* over to the *Olympic* to help bolster that ship because they felt so great about how well the *Titanic* was operating. A gentleman named Captain Smith was one of the resources redeployed to the *Olympic*, and he actually took the key to the locker that held the binoculars for the crew. When they eventually hit the iceberg that sank the *Titanic*, it happened because there were dependencies and interdependencies between these two sister ships. Because someone took the key to the locker that had the binoculars, the crew couldn't look out far enough to avoid the iceberg. And we know the rest of the history."

"I had never heard that," I said.

"Amazing, right?"

"Another thing that we have to think about when we're managing the portfolio and dealing with risk is the risk categories," he continued. (See Figure 9.7.) "In project management, we may have technical risks, or we may have technical debt that we have to deal with, or we may have business risks. At the portfolio level, we have portfolio risk; we have organizational risk, performance risk, resource risk, financial risk, market risk, regulatory risk, reputation risk, quality risk, and contract risk. All of these types of risks impact the portfolio because there are so many more moving parts. The portfolio is impacting the entire organization because they're investing a lot of money. Most portfolios for even a mid-sized company will run into the millions, and larger

Categories
Portfolio Risk
Organizational Risk
Performance Risk
Resource Risk
Financial Risk
Market Risk
Regulatory Risk
Reputation Risk
Quality Risk
Contract Risk

Figure 9.7   Risk categories.
Credit: Mikael Damkier / Adobe Stock

companies have to invest billions of dollars in bringing a new product to market, to improve technology, and so on.

"In regard to portfolio management risk response," he explained (see Figure 9.8), "the goal is to select the optimal choice to minimize the threat and impact a risk could have at the portfolio level or take advantage of the opportunity that event may present. On the opportunities side, we want to do things like exploit the opportunity, share the opportunity, enhance the opportunity, or accept the opportunity.

Figure 9.8   Portfolio management risk response.

And on the threat side, we want to avoid the risk, transfer the risk like insurance, or mitigate the risk with the plan to keep it from happening, and have trigger points where we understand if that risk is there."

In my head, I was already thinking of the work that needed to be done in this time of crisis. Even though it was a lot, I felt ready and prepared to meet the challenge.

"Finally, you must continue through your governance meetings, whether it's monthly or weekly project meetings and monthly portfolio meetings, review the top risks on a regular basis with the leadership team, and bring them up to speed on the risks that have the highest impact that could impact the organization. That's one way to keep risk management in front of people and in front of executives and get them talking about it. And the more you do that, the more people become aware of it, and they start looking for ways to address that on a regular basis instead of waiting for the trigger to happen."

"You have given me so many tools to work with; I'm ready to go."

"No one can really predict a crisis, Jerry, but here we are. I feel confident that you will be able to manage this. Remember, I am a phone call or even a video call away."

"Thank you for everything," I replied. "I mean it."

After we ended the call, I went to the fridge and retrieved a cold beer. I deserved it. My muscles began to unknot as I listened to the kids in their rooms on their school calls. My phone dinged to let me know I had gotten a new email. It was an introduction to Dr. Richardson's lawyer friend. I was both relieved and terrified. Perhaps I needed to use Pugh's matrix to determine what I needed to do for my family. It couldn't hurt.

Dr. Richardson's Tips

- Risk management is the cumulative effect of the probability of uncertain occurrences on certain events that may positively or negatively affect project objectives or the portfolio, and risk can be positive or negative.

- At the portfolio level, we have portfolio risk; we have organizational risk, performance risk, resource risk, financial risk, market risk, regulatory risk, reputation risk, quality risk, and contract risk.
- In regard to portfolio management risk response, the goal is to select the optimal choice to minimize the threat and impact a risk could have at the portfolio level or take advantage of the opportunity that the event may present.

CHAPTER 10

CHOOSING YOUR IMPLEMENTATION STRATEGY

I sighed as I flipped through my emails. The pandemic had impacted everyone, and as upbeat as I tried to be, it was hard. I stayed positive for my kids and for the musicians. The world had changed so much that I was worried it had become the new normal.

The symphony had to cancel two concerts, and the quartet had been stuck because they couldn't fly home. They were supposed to teach, play in the symphony, and also have a chamber music series. None of that was happening, and I was having a hard time with the board. They wanted to cancel the musicians' contracts, but that would strand them, unable to go home. It could cause issues with their visas as well.

I finished my coffee and got ready for a call with Sam. I had a plan that I hoped would work.

"Hey there, Jerry," said Sam when he logged in. "Do you have your arm sling off?"

"Yeah, physical therapy has helped a lot," I replied. "I may even be able to play bass soon."

"Are you kidding? That's great news," he said. "Have you been able to go to their office?"

"Yes, with some pretty tight restrictions," I said. "But my progress has exceeded their expectations."

"That's great," he said. "Listen, I know you're concerned about the quartet."

"I am, but I think I have a plan," I said. "In fact, I think we can get the entire orchestra on board."

"I'm all ears," said Sam.

"I believe we can do concerts with social distancing. They can be spread out on stage, and those who don't play wind or brass instruments can wear masks."

"What about the audience?" Sam said. "The local laws say we can't have a performance."

"We stream it online through one or more platforms. I know it's not optimal, but it is better than having nothing," I said.

Sam scribbled some notes and was silent.

"Can we charge for it?" he asked.

"We could, but the season ticket holders have already paid. The point of the concerts is to keep us in the minds of our patrons. And people are stuck at home and would love an excuse to watch something live."

"I see your point, but how do we monetize it?" Sam asked.

"At this point, we don't. This is a value-added proposition. Right now, we are in survival mode. We have no idea how long this is going to last, nor do we know what things will be like after the restrictions lift, so it's important we don't wait to do something. If we want our patrons to support us, we need to support them through music."

"Okay, I can see that," remarked Sam.

"In addition, I thought we could get the musicians to make some videos individually. They can introduce themselves, talk about their instrument, and even play some excerpts. I have plenty of volunteers all ready to step up to do that."

"They're willing to volunteer?"

"Yes, because not only are they loyal to the symphony, they're trying to figure out what to do during the pandemic. They don't want their skills to go soft, and they're looking for new ways to reach audiences. Many, including me, are giving private lessons virtually. Performing can be a little trickier. But they have cameras and are willing to put themselves out there. In return, the patrons can feel closer to the musicians. We're also considering some live small ensemble performances, such as the quartet in their living room."

"Are you willing to share all of this with the board? While the musicians are willing to volunteer, I feel this falls under marketing and advertising, and so perhaps we can divert funds from those budgets to pay them."

I took a breath. "Really? That would be outstanding."

"Can you get one or two of those videos done and send me the links to share?" asked Sam.

"You bet." We disconnected.

The response from Sam was greater than I had imagined. He had seen the vision and understood the value of what I was proposing. Maybe things weren't as bleak as they seemed.

I looked at my watch. It was time to log on with my therapist. Since being served with papers, I had been on edge. Seeing counselors in person hadn't been possible, but I found an online option.

* * *

"Hey, Jerry, how are things going?" Rachel, my therapist, began the session.

"Well, you know, I'm taking it day by day."

"Anything new this week?"

I told her the good news about my arm and also that things were looking up at work.

"How is virtual school going with the kids?" she asked.

"They are online right now. I don't think they mind it, but it can be frustrating because the teachers haven't been prepared to teach online. Also, they miss their friends. They can call them and see them online, but it's just not the same."

"I get that, but you're doing a great job," responded Rachel. "How are things going with Laura?"

"Frustrating. She doesn't talk to the kids nearly enough. She sometimes forgets calls, and I have to text and remind her. She's in lockdown with her boyfriend, so I guess she's distracted."

"And the divorce, how are you coping with that?"

"Well, it's hard. At first it felt like it came from nowhere, but after working with you, I'm able to see more clearly that things have been headed this way for a long time. I just wanted to make you aware. I do feel guilty about it."

"Why?"

"Because of the kids. They didn't deserve a broken family."

"From your description of them, they seem happier with the situation than in the past. Your son has found music and has connected more with you. And your daughter was heading down a bad road, but because of you she's doing well and seems more stable."

"Yeah, that's true, but they need their mom," I said.

"And they have that, Jerry. You're doing everything you can to facilitate time with them. It is Laura's choice beyond that. You can't control that, nor are you responsible."

"I suppose you're right, but I feel like if I had done something sooner. . . ."

"You can live in a world of 'what if' if you choose. But there is nothing you can do about the past. You can only control what you do right now."

"You're right . . . I get it."

"Have you considered dating?"

I laughed. "Well, it's a little tough in the current situation."

"Yeah, but after we get through the pandemic, will you be open to other people coming into your life again?"

"To be honest, I don't see myself active in the dating scene. But I suppose if I met someone, I would be open to dating. Right now, my focus is on work and the kids. And I really want this divorce to be finalized. Everything has been delayed in the courts."

"I can understand your frustration. Honestly, it sounds like you're doing the best you can in extraordinary circumstances. Try to take time for yourself and be mindful. It's hard when you are working, living, and parenting all in the same space all day. But it will help your anxiety to do something for yourself."

"I have been on the treadmill every day," I offered.

"That's great. Exercise can help in many ways – both physically and mentally. Have you considered yoga?"

"No," I admitted.

"Think about it. It's something you can do at home. There are many apps and videos you can use."

We wrapped up our call, and she gave me some suggestions for yoga apps. As usual, I felt better after the session.

"Dad, I'm hungry," I heard from down the hall. It was dinnertime. No rest for the weary.

★ ★ ★

"It sounds like things are going well," said Dr. Richardson on our video call.

"As well as can be expected," I said.

"I really like the plan you came up with for the musicians," he said. "This week, I want to talk to you about portfolio management implementation and adoption. It's all about project and program execution to get your portfolio started and set up. You've already done some of this, but I hope you learn something new that can help you as you shift to new projects due to the pandemic."

"I'm ready to go!" I said.

"We've gone through a lot as we've talked about portfolio management. We've talked about why to use it and some of the how-tos around the concept. Now I want to talk about setting up your PMO, and again, remember that the PMO could be a project PMO, a program PMO, or a portfolio PMO. So at this time, we're talking about the portfolio PMO."

"Got it," I said.

"So where do you start, and how do you get there?" Dr. Richardson began. (See Figure 10.1.) "You really want to start from the bottom up. You want to capture the projects that are in flight and how much work is going on in the organization. When I first joined the international law firm, I went and met all the senior leaders within the IT group just to get a good handle on the different projects between New York, Boston, and the DC office, even over in Europe. Everyone had a list in their back pocket, but they weren't all open and sharing their lists across the organization. When I consolidated them, instead of having seventy projects going on, there were two hundred to three hundred projects on the list, and many were duplicates, but they weren't all talking to each other, so they didn't know. I know you have these new projects you want to implement. Do you know what else is going on at the symphony right now?"

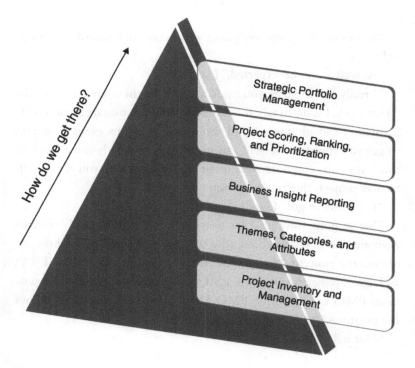

Figure 10.1   Where should you start?

"You know, I don't," I admitted. "But after this call, I am going to find out. I am so siloed here; I don't even think to ask."

"Getting that project inventory is critical, and then you can go from there," Dr. Richardson continued. "You want to categorize the inventory and decide if there are themes and categories. Do you remember the categories we talked about before?"

"Yes."

"These are about how to transform the business, to grow the business, and run the business. And it includes themes like strategic planning, operational excellence, knowledge sharing, and revenue-generating so that you can grow the business. These are the things I am sure are on everyone's mind at the symphony right now, and it's important for them not only to understand what you're doing, but what others are doing in the organization."

"Makes total sense," I replied.

"Back to my story about the law firm. We went through this process and got business insight around reporting. Once we got all this information in the system, we were able to get some reporting going on and start getting business insights, and then we started the project portfolio measure piece, where we began ranking and scoring the projects, prioritizing and recalibrating. And by the time I went back into consulting, we were meeting and taking the strategic plan, working with the enterprise architecture, and marrying the organization's strategy with their project portfolio measurement capability. It was amazing to see how many projects we were able to get done. All the business analysts who were project managers became PMPs. The executive team had amazing visibility into the projects, and we were able to get a lot of work done for the business because now we were able to prioritize their projects and really move them ahead."

"You think I can do that with the symphony?"

"Absolutely. Sharing is the key, and then you can work together rather than, as you put it, in silos."

Dr. Richardson shared a diagram. (See Figure 10.2.)

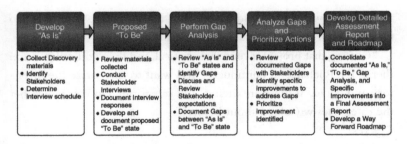

Figure 10.2   PPM 360 assessment.

"Now, something else you need to think about is conducting a project management 360 maturity assessment of your environment, and here's why. If you went to a doctor who had you open your mouth, took your blood pressure, took your temperature, gave you a prescription, and wrote things up without actually doing any kind of blood work or really checking your vitals, you would be very suspicious of that doctor. They're trying to treat you when they really don't know what's going on. They really need to give you a full physical and do blood work. They need to do a stress test or whatever they have to do to get to the root of what's going on."

"True."

"The project portfolio management 360 assessment is like having a diagnostic exam on your portfolio and on the organization. Because in this environment, you're able to capture your as-is, your to-be, to do a gap analysis, and the to-be is basically: where do you need to be able to deliver the types of products and programs and capabilities that the organization needs the project management group to deliver? Remember, the portfolio management practice is like the corpus callosum to the brain of the organization. The corpus callosum allows the right and left hemispheres to communicate, and the portfolio management framework and process, if it's done correctly, allows the strategic plan, which is vision and goals and objectives, to connect to projects and programs, which is the execution and getting things done and tactical work."

I was writing notes. I knew that it was all being recorded but making notes helped me think and process what he was saying.

"And then you want to analyze the credit gap analysis, analyze that gap and really develop that roadmap," he said. "And from this you develop a roadmap of activities, and then usually it turns out to be a one-year or a two-year roadmap. I've even worked with organizations where it turned into a three-year roadmap because they had so many things that needed to change, and they couldn't change them all at one time. And again, you have to consider the culture. Here's a link for a free test drive of a Project Portfolio Management 360 assessment if you'd like to try it."

"Yes, thanks," I said, making note of the link (https://principlesofex ecution.nsvey.net/ns/n/PMO360.aspx).

"You're going the right route by working through Sam and the board as directly as you can. On all of my projects that have gone well, I had a very strong executive who championed the work. When the project didn't go well or even got killed – and that has happened to me – I had to learn some lessons early on from that. Sometimes it happened because I didn't have a strong connection to an executive or I didn't know how to onboard to help them buy in.

One of the ways to get the executives to buy in is you have to poll them and figure out their main points. Other times you have to learn to speak their language and give them what they need."

"I'm trying," I said.

"And you are succeeding. At the law firm, when we first started to try to roll out the portfolio solution, the executives thought I just wanted to spend money, so they shut the project down and said I didn't bring enough evidence to show them that they really needed to go this direction. I went back and did some homework, read a couple of books on the subject, and figured out how to present it to them in a way that they could see, feel, and smell the pain that they were in because they were oblivious to it. When you're at a high-level firm and things are going well, you're so far removed from the challenges that you don't see them. I had to rewrite my charter; I onboarded a consulting group because I knew I couldn't do it all by myself – I was still doing a lot of the day-to-day work of managing my portfolio and managing my team."

"I understand that," I said. "I have that to do, plus all of the other duties I am juggling."

Dr. Richardson continued, "I needed to develop charts to show that if an area was focused around a capability and if a capability didn't have the technology, or it didn't have people who were trained in it, or didn't have a tool to support it, or didn't have the process documented, that process was red. When we looked at all of the processes that make up the portfolio management framework, I would say more than two-thirds of their processes were red and yellow. And when I demonstrated it by showing them that chart, they saw they were really good at financial management and at project execution, but portfolio management, demand management, and all the other parts of the portfolio management framework they were really bad at, but they didn't see that until I displayed the chart and I explained it to them." (See Figures 10.3 and 10.4.)

Note to self: *Develop a chart before the board meeting.*

"That helped them to get on board. And once they got it, the CIO jumped on board as the champion, and that charter got approved.

Figure 10.3   Obtaining executive buy-in.
Credit: insta_photos/Adobe Stock Photos

Capabilities	Demand Mgt	Portfolio Selection	Portfolio Tracking	Portfolio Reporting	Financial Planning	Financial Tracking	Benefits Realization	Project Scheduling and Tracking
Overall								
People								
Process								
Technology								
Governance								

Legend
- Capability implemented
- Capability implemented but limited
- Capability not implemented

Figure 10.4   Conduct a capability assessment.

We were able to deliver the portfolio solution and really help the firm go to another level. But it took learning in that situation and showing them their pain to help create the buy-in.

"Jack Welch once said, 'Good business leaders create a vision, articulate the vision, passionately own the vision, and relentlessly drive it to completion. And they do it by sharing their vision.' All the great companies have leaders who tell stories about why they started the business, or why they do what they do, and they share their heart, and the organization takes on the character of the leader."

I wrote the quote down to ponder more later.

"Because you love music and the symphony, you can see the power and the great things that a strong project portfolio management solution can provide them and how it can really impact the organization in amazing ways. It does require you to have passion and share your vision – getting that sponsor or executive buy-in and getting them to share the vision, and then getting them to tell their story of why they're on board. So your meeting with Sam was spot on. There's so much more emotion in business than people realize, but people are motivated by passion and by someone who has a good why. It's kind of like what Simon Sinek says, 'If you start with why, the how and the what begin to take care of itself.'"

I had heard the quote before, and it definitely held true for the symphony.

Dr. Richardson showed me a chart to use for conducting a gap analysis (see Figure 10.5) and told me, "I really like this chart because you look at the current capability or the current state of the environment, and you basically ask the questions for the current state: What happened? Where's the confusion? When is it done? How does it work, and how is it sequenced? And for the future: What should it look like? Where will it change? When will it change? Who will do this? And how will it be timed and resourced? When you get to the gap analysis section, you're asking questions such as: What's the difference between the current state and the future state? Where will it be different? When are the differences needed? Who will identify and validate the gap? And how will the gap be improved? And for the actions to close the

	What	**Where**	**When**	**Who**	**How**
Current State	What happened?	Where is the confusion?	When is it done?	Who does the work?	How is it sequenced?
Future State	What should it look like?	Where will it change?	When will it change?	Who will do this?	How will it be timed and resourced?
Gap	What is different?	Where will it be different?	When are the differences needed?	Who will identify and validate the gap?	How will the gaps be improved?
Actions to Close Gap	What will be done to address the gap?	Where will it be addressed?	When will it be addressed?	Who will make the decision and complete it?	How will it be rolled out?

Figure 10.5 Conduct a gap analysis.

gap, you want to ask these questions: What will be done to address the gap? Where will it be addressed? When will it be addressed? Who will make the decision and complete it, and how will it be rolled out?"

"So gap analysis is about insight between the current and the future portfolio state?" I asked.

"You've been paying attention," Dr. Richardson chuckled. "By conducting a gap analysis on your current environment and comparing your current and future capabilities against industry best practices, you are able to identify critical processes that can be implemented to improve the organization. And many times, you find a lot of quick wins or a number of quick wins where things are half-baked, or you don't have the document fully done, or the person didn't complete the training, and you can take advantage of those quick wins and start seeing improvement in your organization immediately."

"Let's go back to the chart on the capability assessment I showed you earlier," he continued. "This is the document I came up with when I had to redo the charter. It looks at each of the portfolio management processes and asks what the overall score is. From a people standpoint, have people been trained in this particular area? Like demand management, portfolio selection, or portfolio tracking? Are there processes? Are there documented steps and processes that people can follow? Are we using technology? Not just spreadsheets, but are we using automation and technology to make the process easier? And is there a governance process that can help support that particular capability? As you can see, you may be all green on project scheduling and financial tracking, and even portfolio reporting or requests, but when it comes to demand management, portfolio selection, and so on, you can see that there are some serious gaps there, and for an executive, this is a perfect way to be able to show them that there are some gaps in what we're doing."

"In our earlier talks, we discussed the development of a portfolio strategic plan, but I think it is worth reviewing," he said. (See Figure 10.6.) "This is not the same as the strategic plan for the organization or the strategic plan for the business. This is a strategic plan

> ➤ Portfolio Vision and Objectives
> ➤ Organizational Structure and Area
> ➤ Measureable Goals and Guidance
> ➤ Allocation of Funds
> ➤ Portfolio Benefits, Performance Results, and Value Expected
> ➤ Communication Required to Ensure Successful Change and Implementation
> ➤ Key Assumptions, Constraints, Dependencies, and Risks
> ➤ Portfolio Prioritization Model, a High-Level Prioritization, Decision-Making Framework

Figure 10.6 Develop a portfolio strategic plan.
Credit: olly/Adobe Stock

for the portfolio management office and how you're going to leverage portfolio management skills and tools and techniques and training and business models and risk and communication – all the things that you've been learning. How are you going to strategically roll these out? What's the vision and objective for the portfolio itself? How are you going to structure the organization when we talk about the operational models? What about measuring goals and guidance? We talked about governance, funding, allocation of funding, the portfolio assessment, and how you are going to go about funding projects. How are you going to manage the portfolio benefits, performance results, and value expectations?"

"Those are the questions that have kept me up some nights," I said.

"It shouldn't stress you out. You are doing an outstanding job. I just want to make you aware of some of these things. Some other questions surround communication requirements. When they're successful implementations, and when there are changes, how are you going to handle the cards? The constraints, the assumptions, the risk, and dependencies. And then what are the portfolio prioritization model and the decision framework that you're going to adopt? Are you going to use an analytical hierarchy processing? Are you going to look for something else? Are you going to use an enterprise solution? Are you going to try to do it on a spreadsheet? All of that has to be thought through and thought out, and I know you are already doing that. Trust me, and you are ahead of the curve; I just don't want you to miss anything."

"I get it," I replied.

"There are just a couple of final things I want to go over. First, are there steps for setting up a portfolio management office? In your current position, this may not be relevant, but you've shown interest in perhaps using these skills in bigger organizations in the future." (See Figure 10.7.)

"Absolutely," I replied. As the pandemic dragged on, I might be looking for other employment sooner rather than later.

"First, you want to create a portfolio management strategic plan and a charter, and you want to get those signed off on by the executive team so that they get on board. You want to develop a portfolio management framework and a plan. You want to set up an enterprise portfolio organizational chart where you have the operational body; you want to do a WBS of the things that need to be done. Work breakdown structure, you need a budget and a plan; you need

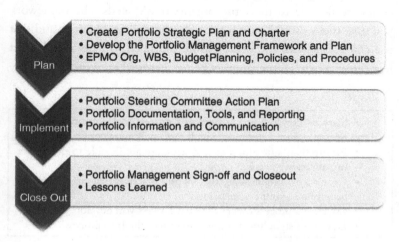

Plan
- Create Portfolio Strategic Plan and Charter
- Develop the Portfolio Management Framework and Plan
- EPMO Org, WBS, Budget Planning, Policies, and Procedures

Implement
- Portfolio Steering Committee Action Plan
- Portfolio Documentation, Tools, and Reporting
- Portfolio Information and Communication

Close Out
- Portfolio Management Sign-off and Closeout
- Lessons Learned

Figure 10.7   What are the steps for setting up a PMO?

policies and procedures. You also need to set up a portfolio steering committee with an action plan. And you also need to document your portfolio management process. You need tools; you need reports; you need portfolio information and a communication strategy. Then you also need portfolio management sign-offs and closeouts and a lessons learned portal. The steps are there to help you get to the next level and really help you to grow and be able to meet the business needs and be aligned with your organization.

"The last thing I'd like to discuss is establishing your project portfolio management practice. The first tip to establish in your PPM practice is developing a streamlined process. Keep it simple at first. Have a process, but make it streamlined because if it's too complicated and difficult, most organizations will not adopt it. And that will usually be because it's harder to get the executives to buy in when it's not streamlined and they don't see the benefit to the business or to themselves personally. You've done an excellent job streamlining what you've done with the symphony. Just think back at where you started and where you are now."

"I really don't want to think about where I started; it was a mess!"

"But now it isn't," he replied. "You need to ensure that the processes are flexible to meet the organization's needs. The framework you give them should only be one they're willing to adopt and that is a cultural fit with the organization. You need to have a document repository where all the projects being managed are visible. Visibility

---

- Start by developing a streamlined process focusing on collaboration, and then determine which tools will meet your needs.
- Ensure that your processes and structure are flexible to meet your organization's needs.
- Create a document repository of best practices that are available to everyone in your organization.
- Establish a process owner for each process you develop.
- Develop a straightforward portfolio recalibration process.

Figure 10.8   How to establish a PPM practice.

creates accountability. You'll need ownership processes and an executive champion to provide support. And then you need a straightforward process for recalibration.

"Remember, recalibration of the portfolio is something that happens on a quarterly basis. It's something that you want to do; again, it could be monthly, it could be quarterly, but if there are changes in the market, new products coming in, you want to be aware of that and be able to know that the products that are in the portfolio may not be the right ones and that you have the ability to adjust those projects and still see the value and benefits that you're trying to create. You also have to have the courage to address those because sometimes you have to say, 'I'll make a recommendation that a project needs to be killed. Not just put on hold but terminated,' and it doesn't map to the strategy because the strategies change."

"Even though I've been buried in stuff, I have tried to establish a schedule."

"It will come," he said. "Just keep working at it until it becomes a habit. Finally, we want to develop a maturing PMO. We want to ask questions like: Are we investing in the right things? Are we optimizing our capacity? How well are we executing our projects? Can we absorb all the changes we are implementing? Do we realize the expected returns and benefits? Realize that there are levels of maturity for accomplishing this, and it doesn't happen overnight; it's an incremental process that takes place."

"Yes, all of those things are critical right now," I said.

"That's all I have for today. Again, I can't emphasize enough how impressed I am that you have improved your portfolio management practices and understanding. Especially in light of everything else going on in your life and in the world."

"I can't thank you enough. I'd still be floundering and arguing with people and would probably have quit or been fired by now. Take care of yourself."

As we hung up the call, I walked to the corner of my office. I unlatched the oversized case of my bass, and for the first time in months, I drew my bow across the strings. Ouch – was it out of tune!

Dr. Richardson's Tips

- By conducting a gap analysis of your current environment and comparing your current and future capabilities against industry best practices, you are able to identify critical processes that can be implemented to improve the organization. And many times, you find a number of quick wins where things are half-baked, or you don't have the document fully done, or the person didn't complete the training. You can take advantage of those quick wins and start seeing improvement in your organization immediately.

- First, you want to create a portfolio management strategic plan and a charter, and you want to get those signed off on by the executive team so that they get on board. You want to develop a portfolio management framework and a plan.

- The first tip to establish in your project portfolio management practice is developing a streamlined process. Don't make it too complicated. Keep it simple at first. Streamline the process, because if it's too complicated and difficult, most organizations will not adopt it.

CHAPTER 11

REAPING THE BENEFITS OF YOUR CHOICES

Time has passed. Jerry meets someone new at his regular coffee shop. They agree on one date. The kids' school year is winding up, and they make plans to spend a good part of the summer with Mom. Laura is seeing someone new.

The calendar on the wall taunted me with the days left until Easter. Winter had been stressful, but nothing compared to the upcoming spring season. The news had come last week that restrictions on public gatherings were beginning to lift. It was both a blessing and a time to panic.

Everything that had been up in the air was now greenlighted. This was great news for the musicians but not such great news for me. I had to scramble to find musicians for upcoming concerts quickly, not only for the symphony but for many of the churches and even the local junior college. Everyone wanted full ensembles, and I had been on the phone and email like a madman for a week.

Just when I thought I had everything under control, I got a call from the choral director, Dawn, who was in charge of the big performance at the cathedral. It was a full 200-member chorus along with a full symphony doing Handel's *Messiah*. We had two performances, and logistically it had been a nightmare.

"Jerry, I hate to let you know this late, but we just got confirmation that the concerts are going to be televised by the local public television station," said Dawn.

I almost dropped the phone. "You're kidding!?"

"No, but I think we should be fine," replied Dawn. "They will be filming at the dress rehearsal, and then they'll be there on Saturday night and Sunday afternoon."

"Okay," I said hesitantly. I was waiting for the other shoe to drop.

"They'll be televised live on Saturday night. So we'll have to pause between pieces for station breaks."

That meant a longer performance. Some of the musicians weren't going to like that. Some of them were older and didn't want to have to drive late after a performance.

"Also, on Thursday and Sunday, they will film and piece all of the performances for a taped show that they'll televise the rest of the month," Dawn continued. "This means we'll have to start an hour earlier for a soundcheck, and they need to be dressed for a performance."

There was the shoe. Many of the musicians had day jobs, so getting there early would mean they wouldn't have time for dinner. Again, they wouldn't be happy.

"Also, since Thursday will be essentially a performance to an empty church, we've asked for people to come to hear it because that will change the hall's acoustics. This means the musicians can invite up to two people to come for free."

That would make the musicians a little happier as the performances had sold out in a couple of hours.

"Now comes the bad news," said Dawn. "We will need to have an extra rehearsal on Wednesday. We will, of course, pay them for the time, but we will need to have everyone there. Will that be a problem?"

Of course that was going to be a problem. The musicians had other rehearsals that week and other obligations.

"I'm afraid I can't guarantee that everyone will be there," I said. "But what I will do is to fill in the missing chairs for that rehearsal. I'm sorry, that will be the best I can do this late."

"I understand," said Dawn. "I know all of this is last minute, and I appreciate your help."

"One thing I will request for Thursday is that we should provide food for the musicians on Thursday night. Many of them won't be able to get home before they have to make it to rehearsal."

"That will be no problem. Again, I appreciate all that you do."

★ ★ ★

"We're ready to go," said Linda.

I was double- and triple-checking that I had everything. Music. Check. Bow. Check. Bass. Check-check. Personnel book. I couldn't forget that. I had been building it for months. It had papers for people to sign, numbers of musicians, and more. While I had a lot of the information accessible on my tablet, I felt safer having paper copies of things.

I moved my arm around a few times. I had had a physical therapy session this week, and it seemed to be holding up. I would know better by the end of the weekend if it had the endurance it once did. I had stepped down from first chair to third for this concert. I had too many other things to keep up with. While I enjoyed playing first chair, it made more sense to hand that duty over until the end of the season.

I walked into the living room with my gear, ready to go.

"I really appreciate this," I said. "This is your mom's weekend, after all."

"We really enjoy seeing you play, Dad," said Corey. "Maybe in a few years, I can play with you."

"I'd really like that," I said.

"Besides, Mom doesn't really like classical music, and we do. It makes the holidays feel more . . . like the holidays," said Linda.

"Well, it's nice to have you in the audience," I said. "It may be a bit chaotic tonight. I probably won't be able to talk to you all until the end."

"No problem," said Corey.

We loaded the car and arrived thirty minutes before the concert. There was a nice spread of food in the rectory. Dawn had come through.

"Go ahead and grab a bite," I said. "I need to see how the setup is going."

It wasn't going well. It was chaos. The floor was covered in cords that led to bright lights as well as large microphone stands. There was a rumbling sound coming from the back of the church.

I tracked Dawn down.

"What is that sound?" I asked.

"It's the trucks outside that will be feeding the satellite feed," she said with a grimace.

"That's not going to work," I said. "No one will be able to hear us. And those cords are a hazard, not to mention those lights in people's eyes."

"You're welcome to talk to Shirley, the producer. She's over there in the blue shirt. If you can take care of that stuff, I'd appreciate it," said Dawn.

"I'm on it," I said. My first priority was the safety and comfort of the musicians.

I approached Shirley and introduced myself.

"How can I help you, Jerry?" she asked in an almost dismissive tone.

"The cords are going to be a problem for some of the musicians," I said. "Is there anything we can do about them?"

She sighed. "I guess. What do you suggest? We need those for the mic booms and the lights."

"Perhaps tape them down or put some carpets over them," I suggested. "I don't want any of my musicians falling. Some are older, and the instruments we carry in some cases are priceless."

Her eyebrows went up. That got her attention.

"Yes, we can fix that," she said. "Anything else?"

"Well, the lights are going to be a problem, and so is that camera there," I pointed. "The musicians have to see the director. Is there any way we could put them at a different angle so that it isn't straight in their eyes when they're looking up?"

"I suppose, but I don't think we can have all that done before you play tonight," she said.

"Tonight isn't live, though, right?" I asked.

"No, but we need as much footage as possible," she replied. "We can have the lights fixed by tomorrow night. I suppose we won't need them all on tonight."

She began to turn away, and I said, "One last thing. That noise. Those generators. We can't have them going on during the performance."

"Well, we need them on to power the trucks, so I'm afraid I can't help you there."

She wasn't very helpful or pleasant. But I wasn't going to give up.

"Do they need to be right near the back door?" I asked. "If you park off to the side, I don't think the noise will penetrate the hall."

"We asked about that," said Shirley. "We were told by the church we couldn't park where you are suggesting because of the grass."

She didn't give me a chance to continue. She walked off.

I looked around the hall until I found the person who could help me.

"Father Russo," I said.

"Oh hi, Jeremy," the priest said with his hand outstretched. "It is so nice to see you."

"You as well, Father," I said. "Listen, we're in a little bit of a bind. We need the television trucks moved from the back of the hall. The producer said they weren't allowed to park on the grass. Can you help me?"

Father Russo frowned. "It has been raining, and those trucks are big. We don't want them tearing up the ground."

I was trying to think fast.

"We could put some cardboard down; then they could park the trucks on that. I can understand your concern. It's that just this program is very important. We haven't done a large ensemble program since this pandemic broke out. Not only will the hall be full, but this is being televised all over the state. It will showcase your beautiful church. Can't you make an exception?"

Father Russo sighed. "I see what you're doing."

I gave him as innocent a look as I could.

"I will allow it," he continued. "But please make sure they take every precaution not to tear up the sod."

"I will personally see to it," I said.

I looked around for Shirley, and I called to her while waving my hand. She didn't seem glad to see me.

* * *

Three days after the concerts, I waited in the coffee shop for Dr. Richardson. He indicated this might be our last session. The spring semester was ending, and he and his wife were going on a long cruise.

"Hey, Jerry," Dr. Richardson said as he sat down with his coffee. "Wow, it's been some time since we've been able to meet face to face. How have you been?"

"My arm is a little sore from the weekend, but I can't complain," I said.

"We saw it on Saturday night. Wow, what a performance."

"I'm so glad you liked it. There was a lot of behind-the-scenes work that made it happen," I said.

"Tell me about it."

I brought him up to speed on what had happened on Thursday night. By Saturday night, the lights were in the right place, and thankfully no one tripped. There were a couple of tire marks in the grass, but Father Russo wasn't too concerned.

"Once all the preliminary stuff was done, it went smoothly," I said.

"Sounds like you did an outstanding job. Bravo," he said, and clapped my back.

"Thanks."

"Like I said on the phone, this will be our last session. You can, of course, contact me when you run into problems, but I have been impressed with your progress. You just need to continue to trust your instincts because they're good."

"I appreciate that," I replied.

"There isn't much in the form of new material, but I want to review what we've gone over these past few months."

- What is portfolio management?
- Portfolio management processes
- Strategic management
- Governance
- Performance management
- Communication management
- Risk management
- Portfolio management implementation and adoption

Figure 11.1   Summary of training.

"I want you to remember that we've covered the portfolio, strategic management process, portfolio governance, performance management, communication management, and risk management.

"We have three different types of process groups. We have a defining process group, aligning process groups, and authoring process groups. And we have a total of sixteen processes across those three process groups in the five knowledge areas. And each process has a set of inputs, tools, techniques, and outputs."

"That has helped me out tremendously," I said.

"I've been thinking about how you handled the musicians the past few months up until a couple of days ago. You have made them the center, the why of what you do. Keep this in mind as you continue your journey next year. You have the summer coming up again, and it will be time to start over again."

"I am so much more prepared this time," I said. "I have projects prioritized and some suggestions for new positions in the symphony to help take over some of these projects. What I realized about this concert is that while I love playing, I have too many responsibilities and things to do. I don't think I need to do that, and I have some job descriptions ready to present to the board."

"Wow, that's outstanding," Dr. Richardson replied.

"I can't thank you enough for being a friend as well as a mentor. My divorce is being finalized, and you were there when I needed someone to talk to, and I will never forget that."

Knowledge Area	Defining Process Group	Aligning Process Group	Authoring and Controlling Process Group
Portfolio Strategic Management	4.1 Develop Portfolio Strategic Plan 4.2 Develop Portfolio Charter 4.3 Define Portfolio Roadmap	4.4 Manage Strategic Change	
Portfolio Governance	5.1 Develop Portfolio Management Plan 5.2 Define Portfolio	5.3 Optimize Portfolio	5.4 Authorize Portfolio 5.5 Provide Portfolio Oversight
Portfolio Performance Management	6.1 Develop Portfolio Performance Management Plan	6.2 Manage Supply and Demand 6.3 Manage Portfolio Value	
Portfolio Communication Management	7.1 Develop Portfolio Communication Management Plan	7.2 Manage Portfolio Information	
Portfolio Risk Management	8.1 Develop Portfolio Risk Management Plan	8.2 Manage Portfolio Risk	

Figure 11.2   Course summary.

Dr. Richardson looked flustered. "Oh . . . it was nothing. It was my pleasure."

"It's interesting," I commented. "Even though we've been talking about project management in the context of my position, I have been using some of the same concepts to organize my life."

"Oh really?"

"I need to consider selling the house, for example. There are a number of things that need to happen before I can do that, and I have created a project of it, with smaller parts such as painting the garage as part of that portfolio. It's amazing how something so overwhelming can be organized. I even have buy-in from my kids. They're helping me paint and clean and are a part of the process of finding a new house based on mutually agreed-upon criteria."

"It sounds like I need to come back from my cruise early," said Dr. Richardson.

"How come?"

"It sounds like you're ready to take over my position as a professor!"

We both laughed and sipped our coffee.

EPILOGUE

"I'm so glad you accepted my invitation for an after-concert drink," I said, sitting down in the booth of my favorite pub.

"My pleasure," said Dr. Richardson. "I'm sorry my wife couldn't come. She has an early morning."

"I totally understand," I said. "My girlfriend will be by in a little bit. She was at a girl's night out, but she wanted to meet you."

"Girlfriend?" Dr. Richardson's eyebrows raised.

"Yes," I replied. "My divorce was finalized months ago. I wasn't going to be a bachelor forever."

"I keep forgetting that it's been over a year since I've seen you."

"A lot has happened for sure," I said. "I don't even know where to start."

"I can say with all honesty that tonight's concert was one of the best I have heard the symphony play."

"Yeah, our new maestro picked an epic lineup for our season finale."

"Not to sound indelicate, but what happened to Maestro Fernando?" asked Dr. Richardson.

"Well . . ." I began. "The symphony implemented a number of new policies, and the culture shifted. A large number of them were the projects I instigated. It required Fernando to work more closely with the board and the orchestra committee, two things he didn't want to do. I held fast that his only job was to pick the music he wanted and be in charge of all things music. While this was part of his job, he didn't want to work with others or allow others to be a part of what he did. It was mutually agreed upon that at the end of last season, he would bow out gracefully."

"Wow, that is fascinating," Dr. Richardson said as he sipped his drink.

"I helped develop a search committee for his replacement. In the first half of the season, we tried out three different conductors. Both the audience and the orchestra voted on their favorite. Yang was hands down everyone's first choice."

"I agree; he brings a lot of personality to the stage."

"We are very fortunate to have found him. He's young and didn't have as much experience as the other two candidates, but he was the best by a long shot," I said.

"Have there been any other changes?" Dr. Richardson asked.

"Yes, Sam retired earlier this year. We are still in the process of hiring someone, but I believe that we have some great candidates."

"It sounds like you've been busy," commented Dr. Richardson.

"I am, and I'm not at the same time," I replied. "I have a number of projects going on, but I don't feel overwhelmed like I did last year. I am much more organized, and thanks to you, I have a skill set I can call upon."

"I'm so glad to hear that."

"This year, when I met with the board, I had a three-year plan mapped out. They were very impressed and joked about where Jerry had gone. They couldn't believe I was the same person they had begun working with a year before."

"You did the work," Dr. Richardson said.

"Yeah, but I couldn't have done it without your help," I replied. "An they've hired a new librarian to handle the music. She has already scanned all the music we currently own."

"That's what you wanted. That's great."

"You have no idea. When we get in parts now, we have a whole process of scanning and putting them in a folder by section. I send the parts to everyone, and if we have a sub or a new player, music is easy to find and send. I can do it right from my phone."

"That sounds a lot easier."

"It not only saves time, but it also saves money. We're missing a number of parts that have been lost over the years. Some of the music is old and brittle. We don't have to worry about that as much, and we've reduced the number of replacements we're paying for. We saved over a thousand dollars this year."

"Wow, are you kidding?"

"No, and the musicians appreciate not having to wait for it in the mail. Also, if they forget their music at home, we can easily print out a new part."

We ordered some snacks while we waited for my girlfriend to arrive.

"Shandra said she'll be here in ten minutes," I said.

"I can't wait to meet her. In the meantime, can I ask how your family is doing?"

"Great, actually. Laura is getting married next month."

"Really? That was quick."

"I wish her all the happiness in the world. I really do. The kids are in counseling. This divorce hasn't been easy, and I felt they needed someone outside the family for them to talk to. Dr. Crowngold has been a godsend. He has really helped them cope."

"That's good to hear."

"Linda is thinking about college. I can't believe she's a junior now. Time flies. She takes her SATs next month. I'm sure she'll do well. Corey made all-county orchestra this year."

"Congrats," he said. "You must be a proud papa."

"You have no idea," I laughed.

Shandra walked in, and my heart skipped. It did that a lot lately. I didn't want to rush things, but I had realized she was the love of my life and I couldn't imagine life without her. The kids adored her. She supported everything I was doing. She was a pediatric physician with her own practice. I had hit the jackpot.

"So nice to meet you, Shandra," said Dr. Richardson as he stood to greet her.

"The pleasure is all mine. Jerry talks about you all the time," Shandra said as she settled in.

"None of it is true," Dr. Richardson said with a sly smile. "I was framed."

We all laughed.

"You know . . . you are responsible for our meeting," she said.

"I am?"

"Yes. I got to the Laughing Brew every morning, and I saw you two talking a number of times. I was attracted to Jerry, but I saw his wedding ring, so I never approached. Then one morning, Jerry was there alone, with no ring."

"Can you believe she asked me out?" I said.

"Are you telling this story, or am I?" she laughed.

"Oh . . . you do it . . . you do a much better job."

"Thank you," she said. "I sat down, and we started talking. I didn't have much time, but I promised to continue the next morning. This happened a couple of times until he finally got the hint."

I grinned.

"He said, 'Instead of talking tomorrow, how about we have dinner tonight?'"

"Wow, you are a smooth talker," Dr. Richardson said. "So subtle."

"It turns out she was also a symphony patron. She sat on the opposite side of the auditorium, so she didn't ever really see me play. And by the way, you missed the best concert of the season," I said.

"I know . . . I know," she replied. "I promised Angie we would go out and totally forgot it was a concert night."

"You are forgiven," I said, and she kissed me briefly on the lips. There was the heart skip again. We talked for another hour, and finally Dr. Richardson said he had to go.

"It was so nice finally meeting you," Shandra said.

"Likewise," Dr. Richardson said. "You need to keep ahold of this one. Jerry is an extraordinary man, and any girl would be lucky to have him."

"Oh, I intend to," Shandra said, and I felt myself blushing.

I thought about all of the things I had accomplished in the past year and all the changes that had occurred. Last year, I felt trapped and a little hopeless. Now, I felt anything was possible.

IMPLEMENTATION GUIDE

Project portfolio management is an effective decision-making, disciplined, and structured approach designed to achieve strategic goals by selecting, prioritizing, assessing, and managing projects, programs, and other related work based on their alignment and contribution to your organization's strategies and objectives. Taking a project portfolio approach will enable you to categorize, evaluate, and prioritize initiatives and manage your resources to enhance the value of existing investments. This approach will also enable you to align your organization's spending with its business priorities and achieve an optimal balance of risk and reward.

In the portfolio management circle, we have items such as leading a business, business goal alignment, the value of the business alignment, program selection, and portfolio optimization. It's really all about creating business value. We can ask the question: Are all the things that we're doing as an organization delivering the value that the organization needs while delighting its customers and creating raving fans? At the portfolio management level, it is about business processes, which are usually conducted at the highest level of the organization. At this level are the decisions about which products, programs, or other initiatives are undertaken at a given period. Criteria are created to select those initiatives, activities, the active management of those initiatives, and whatever benefits those activities promise. Through this process, you're

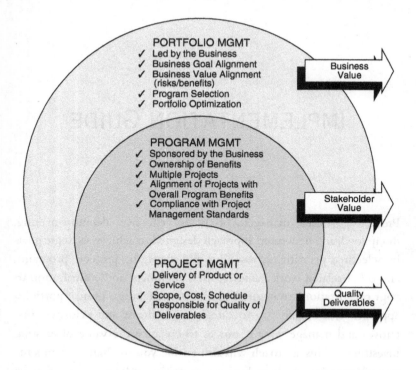

able to realize what those criteria are and trace if the benefits were being delivered.

And also if any projects within the organization need to be terminated. Organizations often struggle with being able to decide whether a project needs to be terminated and instead continue throwing good money after bad because they don't have a process in place to determine what is a bad investment. They don't have anything to compare it to, or they don't have the systems in place.

The portfolio in this story is the symphony. The task of the symphony is to create a season of music for its patrons to enjoy. These include symphony concerts, small ensemble concerts, school programs, and special events like their collaboration with the choral society for their holiday concerts.

At the next level, the program level is what we would call the stakeholder value level. It is where you're thinking of things along the line of sponsors. This happens at the business level, where there are multiple projects that have to be done together. You can't just deliver one of the projects, and everything works; you have to deliver the three, four, five, or even ten products together to get the real benefit to the organization.

It is about who owns the benefits that were promised, that after we invest all this money and deliver all these projects, those projects are going to work.

It's also about the coordination of those projects, because a lot of times those projects are using some of the same resources and some of the same key individuals. And one of the challenges with having poor portfolio management, or program management, is when you start burning out your critical constraint resources, or the people who have the greatest demand and who have really unique skill sets. We can actually burn them out if we don't manage all the work that's coming at them.

At this level, it is also about the alignment of all the projects that are going on and the coordination of management activities across a series of projects over time. And in order to accomplish the overall business goal and objectives that an individual project couldn't do by itself. All those products together deliver some benefit to the organization and its stakeholders; there needs to be some kind of governance process in place to manage all of that. And that's not at the project level or even at the portfolio level; it exists at the program level.

Think of systems that you have at your job where you can't make just one change in one system. If you make a change in one system, then four or five other systems have to be changed as well. That's a program, and if you don't manage it correctly, it can really cause a lot of havoc in the organization.

The programs are the seasonal schedule. What concerts are going to be played, what is the budget for the season, and who will be the soloists and the quartet in residence that year?

At the program level, it's about the benefit of all the products together, and at the portfolio level, it's about the business value that's being created. Finally, there is the project level. This is about delivering quality deliverables, whether that deliverable is a product, a software system, a process document, a solution, an SaaS (software as a service) product, or a symphony concert. The delivery of projects looks at the scope, the cost, and the schedule. It's about being responsible for the quality of the deliverable and the application of knowledge, skills, tools, and techniques to deliver projects on time and on budget.

Finally, there is the project management piece, which is the individual concerts, which is where Jerry will be spending the most time and effort because each concert will have its own challenges. He also has the contracts, hiring, and payroll for each concert to manage as well.

The value of project portfolio management comes from creating positive changes in an organization and how the organization, or the company, performs overall because portfolio management is about managing all those investments, projects, and work that are going on within the organization. Project portfolio management also increases the organization's capability to be more effective and efficient with its resources. It's because you're making more strategic decisions, and you're also making sure that the things that you are investing in are aligned to your strategy, goals, objectives, and where the organization is trying to go. The organization is able to make better decisions and engage with executives to create better executive engagement and employee engagement because the executives know why they invested in the things that they're investing in, and that they are aligned to the strategy, and the employees know that what they're working on is actually going to move the needle.

A report from the Project Management Institute (PMI), "The Pulse of the Profession," is an in-depth dive into portfolio management based on a global survey of more than a thousand project, program, and portfolio managers. They found that 62% of projects that organizations themselves describe as "highly effective in project portfolio management" met or exceeded their expected return on investments of various projects that they selected. Also, among those organizations that described their project portfolio management procedures as "highly effective," 89% of the respondents said, "Senior management under-stands portfolio management at least moderately." In other words, they were much more engaged in the process. A key takeaway from the report was that organizations could obtain the full benefit of portfolio management by making it a fixed part of their day-to-day culture. And really, when you implement portfolio management, it enhances and improves your organization's culture.

The key to making all of these projects work is finding the right people to manage them. The committee that hired Jerry was confident they had hired the right person, and Jerry needed to find competent musicians to hire for the orchestra to produce outstanding concerts.

So once you have a successful implementation of a project port-folio management capability, here are some questions you have to think about:

- Are we investing in the right things?
- Are we optimizing our capacity?
- How well are we executing our projects?
- Can we absorb all the changes we are implementing?
- Are we realizing expected returns and benefits?

You'll want to make sure that the projects are being done properly and that your project management processes are robust enough, but at the same time light enough, not to get bogged down while getting things done, get the project started, get the solutions implemented, get the team on board, and get the solutions and the processes and the deliverables delivered in a timely manner.

One of the things that portfolio management helps organizations with is making sure they're not taking on too much. Think about it like going to a restaurant and ordering everything off the menu; there's no way you can eat it all. Portfolio management gives you that filter that says, "Wait a minute, you can't have the pizza, and the hamburger, and the steak, and the lobster, and the swordfish, and the tofu. There are a few things that you can have, but you can't eat all of them at one time. But maybe you can come back once a week and have something else."

It really helps think about whether the organization can absorb all those changes. Are we really seeing the promised benefits, where everyone says, "Hey if we invest in this project, all these great things are going to happen"? Portfolio management helps you to determine these questions, ask these questions, and develop the answers to these questions.

Jerry had his hands full working through these levels, from portfolio management and program management all the way to project management, while maintaining his position as one of the performers in the symphony. The implementation guide that follows gives you a bottom-up approach. You will find the critical steps and strategies for implementing a portfolio management capability in your organization, just like Jerry did with the symphony.

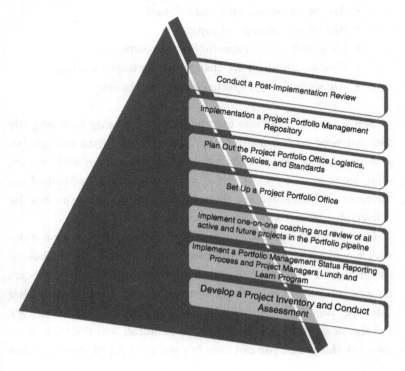

STEP 1: DEVELOP A PROJECT INVENTORY AND CONDUCT ASSESSMENT

The purpose of this task is to create a comprehensive project list of all the projects in your organization, to assess the current state of project management, and to baseline the project management processes and maturity level with the intent to elevate the project management maturity level of the organization. This task includes the following key activities:

- Collect and compile a comprehensive list of all projects in the organization.
- Prepare for the assessment.
  - Define materials to be reviewed based upon the assessment preparation process.
  - Determine appropriate stakeholders to be interviewed.
  - Define the interview schedule in order to establish specific dates, interviewee names, interview location, and specific start and stop times.
- Review materials and conduct assessment interviews.
- Review the materials listed in the assessment preparation document.
- Conduct the interviews according to the agreed-upon interview schedule.
- Document the results of the materials review and interviews in preparation for the next subtask.
- Develop an assessment report and present it to stakeholders.
- Document findings of the current project portfolio management maturity level of the organization and organize them into the project management maturity model.
- Draft an assessment report.
- Perform gap analysis between the current state and the desired future state.

- Prioritize identified gaps.
- Incorporate the sponsor's feedback and produce the final draft of the assessment report.
- Confirm the contents of the final draft of the assessment report with your sponsor(s) and solicit feedback.
- Incorporate final feedback and produce the final assessment report.
- Present the final assessment report to your stakeholders.

STEP 2: IMPLEMENT A PORTFOLIO MANAGEMENT STATUS REPORTING PROCESS AND PROJECT MANAGERS LUNCH-AND-LEARN PROGRAM

The purpose of this task is to implement a weekly status report process with templates to gain a clearer understanding of the key portfolio elements, programs, projects, milestones, deliverables, benefits, risks, and issues that are impacting the project portfolio management environment.

This task includes the following key activities:

- Develop a draft project portfolio management status reporting process and project management status report template.
- Review the draft status report process and templates with the leadership and executive team and solicit feedback. If needed, facilitate prioritization of requirements ("must-have" versus "optional") with stakeholders, and balance those against the deliverables within the scope of the project.
- Incorporate feedback and produce the final project management status report process and template.

STEP 3: IMPLEMENT ONE-ON-ONE COACHING AND REVIEW ALL ACTIVE AND FUTURE PROJECTS IN THE PORTFOLIO PIPELINE

The purpose of this task is to implement and provide one-on-one mentoring and coaching to develop a project portfolio management center of excellence with the current project management team.

This task includes the following key activities:

- Provide expert-level project portfolio management mentoring and coaching to designated group(s) of project managers and stakeholders.
- Assist project managers and stakeholders with the implementation and application of PM industry best practices; with the effective use and adoption of the organization's project management and software development methodologies when developed; and with the integration of best-practice theory, methodology, and tools in an effort to drive consistent delivery of projects, improve project outcomes, and increase organizational project management maturity.

STEP 4: SET UP A PROJECT PORTFOLIO OFFICE

The purpose of this task is to develop a high-level understanding and set the requirements of the key components for the current project portfolio management office environment.

This task includes the following key activities:

- Using the session notes, whiteboards, and flipcharts, draft a document setting out the requirements for a high-level project portfolio office.
- Review the draft high-level project portfolio office requirements document with the sponsor and solicit feedback. If needed, facilitate prioritization of requirements ("must-have"

versus "optional") with stakeholders, and balance those against the deliverables within the scope of the project.

- Incorporate feedback and produce the final high-level project portfolio office requirements document.

STEP 5: PLAN THE PROJECT PORTFOLIO OFFICE LOGISTICS, POLICIES, AND STANDARDS

The purpose of this task is to document and analyze the requirements for an initial set of project portfolio management methodology standards to support the maturation of the organization's existing project portfolio management practices.

This task includes the following key activities:

- Facilitate a series of requirements-gathering sessions with the organization's staff focused on gathering the necessary information so that those requirements can be translated into a draft requirements document for the project portfolio management methodology.
- Develop a draft project portfolio management methodology requirements document from the session notes, whiteboards, and flipcharts. The draft requirements document will specify the processes to be analyzed as well as the documents, templates, and checklist to be developed.
- Review the draft project portfolio management methodology requirements document with the leadership sponsor and solicit feedback. If needed, facilitate prioritization of requirements ("must-have" versus "optional") with stakeholders to ensure that all critical project management processes and procedures are captured.
- Incorporate feedback and produce the final project portfolio management methodology requirements document.

STEP 6: IMPLEMENT A PROJECT PORTFOLIO MANAGEMENT REPOSITORY

The purpose of this task is to configure a pilot project portfolio management solution based upon requirements identified in a configuration requirements process.

This task includes the following key activities:

- Conduct requirements-gathering sessions and document business requirements.
- Perform portfolio solution installation.
- Configure and construct the portfolio solution.
- Conduct training.
- Implement a fully configured pilot solution.
- Perform an online review session of the initially configured solution with the organization, and document appropriate in-scope modifications.

STEP 7: CONDUCT A POST-IMPLEMENTATION REVIEW

The purpose of this task is to review the implemented project portfolio environment and lessons learned throughout the engagement.

This task includes the following key activities:

- Conduct a "lessons-learned" review of the engagement's impact on your organization's project portfolio environment.
- Develop a draft of a lessons-learned document from the session notes, whiteboards, and flipcharts.
- Review the draft of the lessons-learned document with the engagement sponsor and solicit feedback.
- Incorporate feedback and produce the final lessons-learned document.

DR. RICHARD'S LESSONS

LESSON 1, CHAPTER 1: THE RIGHT PEOPLE AND THE RIGHT TIME

- Identify ideal candidates to manage the organization's project portfolio.
- Understand the difference between project, program, and portfolio management.
- Learn about the value portfolio management can deliver to your organization.
- Identify the questions to consider when implementing portfolio management.

The goal in lesson one is to be able to identify ideal candidates to manage an organization's project portfolio. In addition, you'll gain an understanding of the difference between projects, programs, and portfolio management. It is essential to be able to distinguish between a project PMO, a program PMO, and a portfolio PMO because those three are very different in how they operate and their governance processes. The value of portfolio management and how you can deliver that value to your organization cannot be understated. You will learn as a consultant or as a practitioner how to do this, how to deliver value to your client's organization, and the questions to consider when you're implementing the project portfolio management processes.

LESSON 2, CHAPTER 2: CHOOSING YOUR PORTFOLIO, AND CHAPTER 3: SELECTING YOUR PROJECTS

- What is portfolio theory?
- What is a portfolio?
- What is portfolio management?
- What is the role of a portfolio manager?
- Review the history of portfolio management.

In this lesson, you will gain a better understanding of: What is portfolio theory? What is a portfolio? What is portfolio management, and what is the role of the portfolio manager? You will learn some of the histories of portfolio management and how we've gone from where it started to where we are today. Portfolio theory states that for any allocation of resources, there is an efficient set that yields the greatest return for a given level of risk. While the right level of resources to allocate to projects cannot be known without considering further factors, what is clear is that once that level of investment is determined, then an optimal set of projects to implement for a given level of risk and investment can be selected.

LESSON 3, CHAPTER 4: CHOOSING YOUR PORTFOLIO PROCESSES

- Identify portfolio management process groups.
- Learn about strategic planning and the portfolio delivery process.
- Discover organizational strategy and portfolio management.
- Uncover the corpus callosum for the business.

In this lesson, you'll learn to identify portfolio management process groups and understand how strategic planning and portfolio delivery processes work together. You will learn about organizational strategy and portfolio management integration points. You will learn about the corpus callosum, which is a portion of the brain that bridges the right and left hemispheres, and how it helps to explain the concepts of how portfolio management integrates your business.

LESSON 4, CHAPTER 5: CHOOSING YOUR STRATEGY

- Understand the power of strategy links and strategic alignment.
- Learn how to determine the value in business value creation.
- Why are business drivers critical to aligning the project portfolio to the organization's strategy?
- Understand the bridge and hub approach to portfolio management.

Linking portfolio management to strategy balances the use of resources to maximize the value delivered in executing programs, projects, and operational activities. In this lesson, you will learn about strategic management. You will understand the power of strategic links and strategic alignment and learn how to determine the value in business value creation. You'll also learn why business drivers are critical to aligning the project portfolio to the organization's strategy and understand the bridge and hub approach to portfolio management.

LESSON 5, CHAPTER 6: CHOOSING YOUR RULES OF ENGAGEMENT

- What is governance?
- What is a governance framework?
- What are governance policies, processes, and procedures?
- What is the portfolio governance operational model?
- What is the PPM governance decision process?

Governance is the process of putting policies, procedures, and processes in place to guide organizational, operational activities, and change. Governance should provide a streamlined approach and process. If governance becomes a bottleneck, then there's something wrong with the design of the governance processes. The goal of governance is to make things run faster, not to become a bottleneck. In this lesson, you will gain a better understanding of what governance is, what the governance framework is, and what types of policies, processes, and procedures you should create for your portfolio management governance. You will learn what a portfolio governance operational model is and how a project portfolio management governance decision process works. In this lesson, you will look at the five processes that make up the portfolio governance process group: develop a portfolio management plan, define the portfolio, optimize the portfolio, authorize the portfolio, and provide portfolio oversight.

LESSON 6, CHAPTER 7: CHOOSING YOUR PERFORMANCE METRICS

- What is performance management?
- How is performance management implemented?
- What are portfolio management performance metrics?
- Describe portfolio demand and supply.
- Describe the portfolio efficiency frontier.

In this lesson, you'll be able to describe what performance management is, understand what it takes to implement a performance management system, have an idea about portfolio management performance metrics, be able to describe portfolio demand management and supply, and talk intelligently about the efficiency frontier in portfolio management. In performance management, the process groups we're tracking have three processes. The first is to develop a portfolio performance management plan, which is part of the project portfolio management plan. The second is to manage supply and demand. And third is to manage the portfolio value.

LESSON 7, CHAPTER 8: CHOOSING YOUR COMMUNICATION STRATEGY

- What is communication management?
- Discover stakeholder expectation: influence and interest.
- Elicit stakeholder requirements.
- Understand the power of culture.

Selecting a communication strategy is focused on satisfying the most important information needs of stakeholders so that every portfolio decision is made and organizational objectives are met according to the *Standard for Portfolio Management*. In this lesson, you'll learn to understand and communicate what the communication management strategy is, discover stakeholder expectations, learn how to handle influencers and their interests, learn how to elicit stakeholder requirements at a portfolio level, and understand the power of culture and your need for a communication strategy that addresses the current and target company culture.

LESSON 8, CHAPTER 9: CHOOSING YOUR RISKS STRATEGY

- Learn about managing risk.
- Understand portfolio management risk tolerance.
- Identify risk rating (impact and likelihood).
- Find out about the portfolio risk register.
- Recognize Pugh's risk strategy matrix.

Measuring risks is a part of the project portfolio management function both at the project initiation and throughout the life cycle of a project portfolio. In this lesson, you'll be able to manage risk, understand portfolio management risk tolerance, and have a better understanding of risk rating, likelihood, and impact. Receive a copy of a risk register and understand Pugh's risks strategic or strategy matrix.

LESSON 9, CHAPTER 10: CHOOSING YOUR IMPLEMENTATION STRATEGY

- Understand where you should start when developing a project portfolio management office and solution.
- Learn about obtaining executive buy-in.
- What are the steps for setting up a PMO?
- Learn how to establish a PPM practice.

In this lesson, you will learn about portfolio management implementation and adoption. It's all about project and program execution to get your portfolio started and set up. In this lesson, you'll understand where to start when developing a project portfolio management office and solution, how to obtain executive buy-in, find out the steps to setting up a PMO, and learn how to establish a project portfolio management practice.

RECOMMENDED READING AND RESOURCES

ASCENDING TO THE APEX OF THE PROJECT MANAGEMENT LADDER

Demystifying Project Portfolio Management and Building a Winning Game Plan for becoming a PPM Expert: https://geraldjleonard.teachable.com/p/the-apex-of-project-management

This course is designed for project and program managers, PMO executives, decision-makers, consultants, executives, and project team members who have been tasked with oversight, implementation, and operations of their organization's portfolio management capability, and who need to:

- Align a company's project investments with its strategic goals and objectives.
- Gain the skills to better align a selection of projects to the organization's business and strategy.
- Acquire the knowledge to develop and execute a standardized set of best practices for project portfolio management.
- Implement a portfolio management governance program that provides guidance and stewardship over the project ideation, selection, calibration, and execution processes while establishing policies and procedures to effectively manage the company's portfolio assets.

- Improve your career and competitive positioning by enabling the development of skills to help your company to identify and select investments that will capitalize on business values.
- Monitor the organization's portfolio performance.
- Track and perform portfolio management risk monitoring while optimizing the portfolio to mitigate the risk identified.
- Engage stakeholders at all levels of the organization and execute a comprehensive communication strategy.

PMO 360 MATURITY ASSESSMENT LITE

Assessing an organization's capability in project portfolio management requires a systematic framework that you can use to define the nature of your organization's project management processes; an approach that is objective and allows comparisons both within and across industries is required. The PMO 360 Maturity Assessment allows you to define the present state of your organization's project, program, and portfolio management processes.

It takes less than five minutes to complete the assessment, and you will receive a free customized report of your results! https://principlesofexecution.nsvey.net/ns/n/PMO360.aspx

TRANSPARENTCHOICE

Software that transforms the way you make decisions. "Project prioritization" is the foundation for portfolio management. Good prioritization lets you focus on delivering strategic impact, fix the "too many projects" problem, and more effectively plan your resources.

TransparentChoice's software is based on decision science and research into what actually works, so it actually works.

TransparentChoice Home page: https://hubs.ly/Q01dMsHC0

Project Prioritization Ultimate Guide: https://hubs.ly/Q01dMtT10

SIGN UP AT PRODUCTIVITY INTELLIGENCE INSTITUTE™

RESOURCES FOR ACCOMPLISHING MORE EVERY DAY!™

According to a recent survey conducted by the Project Management Institute, "The newly released figures predict that nearly 22 million new jobs will be created during the next decade – and by 2027, employers will need nearly 88 million individuals working in project management-oriented roles."

According to the *Wall Street Journal,* "Burnout on the job is on the rise, to the point where companies have farmed out their workers' well-being to employee assistance programs, where stress and anxiety are cited in 70% of incoming calls."

We believe that professionals who are looking for an edge to be more effective and productive and who want to learn how to stop feeling overwhelmed will benefit from our membership program. We will leverage a human-focused design; they will receive weekly productivity hacks, expert guidance, and perspective, engaging short talks, peer-to-peer accountability, and bimonthly group coaching so that they can learn to be more productive without feeling overwhelmed. https://productivityintelligenceinstitute.com/

GROWTH STRATEGIES MASTERMIND: TOP MINDS HELPING TOP MINDS™

Growth Strategies Mastermind is a 90-day group coaching program. https://productivityintelligenceinstitute.com/mastermind/

I help professionals increase their productivity, reduce stress, and eliminate overwhelm, so they get more done and find more free time for their family and friends. I'm your answer when you need to build your work teams, get everyone working toward the same goal, and grow your business faster.

And I don't just talk about helping you become a transformative growth-oriented leader inside Growth Strategies Mastermind. I go above and beyond to guarantee your success. I do that through my "100% Confidence" Guarantee: In 90 days, you will say with 100% certainty that you possess the knowledge, skills, and tools required to continue leading high-performing teams for the rest of your career while maintaining a safe boundary between work time and family time. Or I'll work with you for an additional 30 days to get you there.

Benefits of the Growth Strategies Mastermind™:

- A supportive and exclusive community of Top Mind Experts.
- A collaborative and synergistic group who freely exchange ideas with each other.
- Healthy discussions with other Top Minds will open your mind to new ideas, options, and big ideas.
- Obtain genuine advice and feedback from experts who have faced the same challenges you're facing.
- Access to a sounding board for testing ideas and who can evaluate your ideas and plans.
- Access to more resources, insights, wisdom, and lessons learned.
- Access to a valuable support network.
- You will gain a new perspective – looking at your challenges through your mastermind members' eyes.
- Gain access to tap into the experience and skills of other Top Mind Experts.
- Access to a diversity of experience and expertise.
- Accelerate the growth of each member – sharpen your business and personal skills.
- Ability to share your current problems, issues, or challenges, making them more tangible and easier to dissect.
- A group of experts that will help hold you accountable.
- Learn how to eliminate limiting beliefs and develop new habits that accelerate your personal and professional growth.

STRATEGY IMPLEMENTATION INSTITUTE

Implementing strategy is a rare and highly appreciated skill set that sets apart the most successful and influential leaders in business.

People with the skill to implement the strategy are in high demand from organizations all around the world. https://www.strategyimplementationinstitute.org/

RECOMMENDED READING AND RELATED HARVARD BUSINESS REVIEW CASE STUDIES

- Chapter 2, "Choosing Your Portfolio," MDCMI, Inc. (B): Strategic IT Portfolio Management, https://hbr.org/product/mdcm-inc-b-strategic-it-portfolio-management/KEL172?sku=KEL172-PDF-ENG
- Chapter 3, "Selecting Your Projects," Peak Experiences and Strategic IT Alignment at Vermont Teddy Bear, https://store.hbr.org/product/peak-experiences-and-strategic-it-alignment-at-vermont-teddy-bear/JIT031
- Chapter 4, "Choosing Your Portfolio Processes," Biocon Research: Preparing for the Bio-Pharmaceutical Transition, https://hbr.org/product/biocon-research-preparing-for-the-bio-pharmaceutical-transition/IMB807?sku=IMB807-PDF-ENG
- Chapter 5, "Choosing Your Strategy," SATS Ltd.: Building Capabilities for the Future, https://store.hbr.org/product/sats-ltd-building-capabilities-for-the-future/w21215?sku=W21215-PDF-ENG
- Chapter 6, "Choosing Your Rules of Engagement," Sony Computer Science Laboratories: Sustaining a Culture and Organization for Fundamental Research, https://store.hbr.org/product/sony-computer-science-laboratories-sustaining-a-culture-and-organization-for-fundamental-research/ke1165?sku=KE1165-PDF-ENG

- Chapter 7, "Choosing Your Performance Metrics," People Analytics at McKinsey, https://store.hbr.org/product/people-analytics-at-mckinsey/418023?sku=418023-PDF-ENG
- Chapter 8, "Choosing Your Communication Strategy," Hindú: Revitalizing a Colombian Tea Brand, https://store.hbr.org/product/hindu-revitalizing-a-colombian-tea-brand/w21014?sku=W21014-PDF-ENG
- Chapter 9, "Choosing Your Risks Strategy," Tristar Hotel Group: Customer Satisfaction and Technology Adoption, https://store.hbr.org/product/tristar-hotel-group-customer-satisfaction-and-technology-adoption/w20840?sku=W20840-PDF-ENG
- Chapter 10, "Choosing Your Implementation Strategy," Technical Note: Putting Discovery-Driven Planning to Work, https://store.hbr.org/product/technical-note-putting-discovery-driven-planning-to-work/kel355?sku=KEL355-PDF-ENG
- Chapter 11, "Reaping the Benefits of Your Choices," Digital Transformation at L&T (B), https://store.hbr.org/product/digital-transformation-at-l-t-b/isb272?sku=ISB272-PDF-ENG

BIBLIOGRAPHY

"APM Receives Its Royal Charter" (January 6, 2017), Association for Project Management, https://www.apm.org.uk/news/apm-receives-its-royal-charter.

Bible, M., and S. Bivins. (2011). *Mastering Project Portfolio Management: A Systems Approach to Achieving Strategic Objectives.* J. Ross Publishing.

Kendall, G., and S. Rollins. (2003). *Advanced Project Portfolio Management and the PMO.* J. Ross Publishing.

Letavec, C. (2006). *The Program Management Office,* illustrated ed. J. Ross Publishing.

Levine, H. (2005). *Project Portfolio Management.* Jossey-Bass.

Morris, P., and A. Jamieson. (2004). *Translating Corporate Strategy into Project Strategy.* Project Management Institute.

Perry, P. (2011). *Business Driven Project Portfolio Management Conquering the Top 10 Risks That Threaten Success.* J. Ross Publishing.

Project Management Institute. *The Standard for Portfolio Management,* 4th ed., 2017.

Project Management Job Growth and Talent Gap Report 2017–2027 (2017), Project Management Institute, accessed October 1, 2018, https://www.pmi.org/-/media/pmi/documents/public/pdf/learning/job-growth-report.pdf?sc_lang_temp=en.

Rollins, S., and R. Lanza. (2005). *Essential Project Investment Governance and Reporting.* J. Ross Publishing.

Sanwal, A. (2007). *Optimizing Corporate Portfolio Management Aligning Investment Proposals with Organizational Strategy.* Wiley.

"Stan Richards's Unique Management Style" (October 1, 2018), Inc., https://www.inc.com/magazine/201111/stan-richards-unique-management-style.html.

"US Senate Unanimously Approves the Program Management Improvement and Accountability Act" (December 1, 2016), Project Management Institute, https://www.pmi.org/about/press-media/press-releases/senate-program-management-act.

ACKNOWLEDGMENTS

I am extremely grateful to the team of John Peragine, John Kremer, George Foster, David Aretha, and my PR team at Smith Publicity for their wisdom, insight, and coaching. I am thankful for my literary agent, John Willig, and my publishing editor, Sally Baker, at John Wiley and Sons.

This book is dedicated to my son, Kenon, and daughter, Peyton, for loving me through my life's journey and personal growth. They have helped me become the man I am today.

To my mom and dad, Lola J. Leonard and Willie C. Leonard, for without your love, compassion, and discipline, I would not know what a hardworking, loving, and compassionate family man is.

To my siblings – Deborah D. Leonard, Sharon L. Stevens, Wendell L. Leonard, the late Harold L. Leonard, and Carolyn Leonard – for protecting me, guiding me, and putting up with me. I love you deeply.

Finally, to my wife, Edith Leonard, for loving me through my journey of bringing this book to life and loving me for who I am.

ABOUT THE AUTHOR

Gerald J. Leonard, PMP, PfMP, and C-IQ Coach, is the publishing editor, CEO, and founder of the Leonard Productivity Intelligence Institute, as well as the CEO of Turnberry Premiere, a strategic project portfolio management and IT governance firm based in Washington, DC. He received a bachelor's degree in music from Central State University in Ohio, and later earned a master's in music from the Cincinnati Conservatory of Music. After graduation, Gerald moved to New York City, where he worked as a professional bassist and studied with the late David Walters, a distinguished professor of double bass at both the Juilliard and Manhattan schools of music.

Gerald earned certifications in project management and business intelligence from the University of California, Berkeley; Theory of Constraints Portfolio Management from the Goldratt Institute; executive leadership from Cornell University; and the Wharton School: Entrepreneurship Acceleration Program and Scaling a Business: How to Build a USD $1 Billion+ Unicorn.

In his leisure time, Gerald loves playing golf, traveling internationally, and playing his upright bass on special occasions.

To learn more about Gerald, visit www.geraldjleonard.com

INDEX